Other books in the *Astro*
[call 1.800.

MW00848772

Volume 1

"What it comes down to is that Blaschke's book is strong enough at several different levels—practical, theoretical, esoteric—that one can find good information in it...I have a feeling that this book, due to its comprehensive treatment of the subject, could easily become a classic."
- Kenneth Irving, American Astrology

"This is the perfect book if you are a practicing astrologer using secondary progressions and maybe dabbling with tertiary and minor progressions...As a practicing astrologer, you are undoubtedly using some of the techniques that the author includes in his book; I am quite sure that even many advanced astrologers have not applied the range and depth of techniques that Robert shares in this book. I highly recommend it." *- Mary Plumb, The Mountain Astrologer*

"Blaschke is an excellent teaching writer. He knows exactly how to introduce his material in small, precisely measured increments, cite his authorities with clarity and brevity, and guide the reader through virtually frustration free assimilation and mastery of progression theory and application. After reading this book and working within the guidelines presented, many of us might begin to wonder why we had not learned these techniques sooner. The answer is that there probably weren't enough teachers or writers of this man's caliber available when we first began the study and practice of astrology." *- Joan Star, Geocosmic Magazine*

Volume II - Sabian Aspect Orbs

"Mr. Blaschke has devised a theory that has not only added an extra level to aspect analysis but has added considerable texture and pliability as well. The book has many attributes that will offer the reader added insight, not just to his theory on Sabian Aspect Orbs, but in general to aspects and their manifestation."
- Scott Whitters, FAA Journal (Australia)

"What the author has uncovered for us is an underlying energy between any two degrees in the Zodiac - no matter what planets may be tenanting them. This precision enables clear distinctions to be drawn between - say - an applying trine of one degree and a separating trine of one degree (or any other combination of aspect and orb). And such precision, which before may have appealed more to the mathematically-minded than the intuitive, is brought out of the abstract realm of measurement and into the colourful realm of meaning by the inclusion of the Sabian symbols. What a wonderful world this opens up. Pictures to explain technical measurements. Right brain married to left. A remarkable achievement, a fascinating book, and an invaluable reference."
- Paul F. Newman, The Astrological Journal (UK)

"The Sabian Aspect Orb provides a new view of the nature of the aspect between two planets. Robert Blaschke is an intricate thinker and an excellent teacher. He, along with Dane Rudhyar, has Jupiter in Gemini; he is thus able to explain simply this somewhat complex subject matter. This book is a natural for the many astrologers who love Sabian symbols and use them in their work. I believe that astrologers who do not especially gravitate to the Sabian symbols will find this book a treasure as well, for its expert teaching on the nature of aspects."
- Mary Plumb, The Mountain Astrologer

"Robert has an ingenious mind, with which he examines the Sabian Symbols in a unique context, that of relating every aspect to a degree meaning. With his usual thorough and clear explanation, he examines the difference between waxing and waning aspects together with their applying and separating pattern."
- Lois M. Rodden, Data News

...dedicated, with love and encouragement, to:
my fellow self-employed astrologers, present and future...

cover art from a commissioned original water color painting
by Sarah Jones   January 2002

Virgo 22°
Upon rich velvet in a case, at an exhibition, is an
exquisitely wrought miniature; a jewel-set royal coat-of-arms.

[Marc Edmund Jones; Lecture~Lessons; 1931]

Astrology
A Language of Life

Volume III
A Handbook for the Self-Employed Astrologer

Robert P. Blaschke

Edited by Anna Raphael

Earthwalk School of Astrology Publishing

Ashland, Oregon USA

First edition published in 2002 by

Earthwalk School of Astrology
PO Box 832
Ashland, Oregon 97520 USA
1.800.778.8490
ewastro@earthlink.net

First printing: March 2002 - 1000 copies

Library of Congress Control Number: 2002101962

International Standard Book Number (ISBN): 0-9668978-2-X

Printed in the United States of America

A portion of the material incorporated in this book was previously published in the form of a book excerpt chapter entitled Teaching Astrology & Becoming A Self-Published Astrological Author in *How to Start, Maintain and Expand an Astrological Practice;* © 2001 by Robert Mulligan; The Organization for Professional Astrology; ISBN 0-9700696-2-6; www.professional-astrology.org; 941.261.2840.

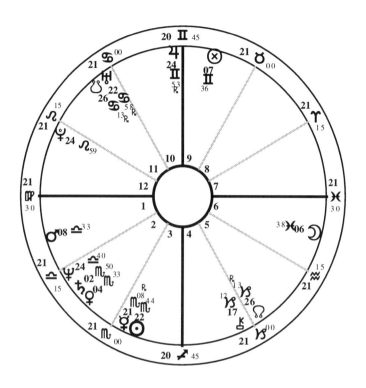

Nativity of the Author

15 November 1953
1:37 AM PST
Santa Monica, California
33N50   118W29
Porphyry Houses
True Node

[from birth certificate]

Table of Contents

Chapter Three

Chapter Four

Chapter Five

Chapter Six

Chapter Seven

Chapter Eight

Chapter Nine

Chapter Ten

Chapter Eleven

Chapter Twelve

Acknowledgments

I want to give special thanks to my editor, Anna Raphael, for the outstanding job she has done going through my manuscript and helping make this a more readable book. It is a challenge to find a person who is both a seasoned astrologer and a good writer, and I am indebted to her for the intelligence, care and years of experience she brought to the examination and improvement of this volume.

I also want to thank Steven Forrest for taking time in the middle of his very busy schedule to write the foreword for this book. He is one of our profession's best role models, an author and lecturer who is also a hard working astrologer with a commitment to quality and integrity. Unbeknownst to me, on the day I called him about the foreword, my progressed Sun was conjunct his Jupiter within three minutes of arc! His Ascendant is also the degree of my Sun. Thank you, my friend.

I am beholden to my colleagues and friends from abroad, Paul F. Newman of the UK, and Scott Whitters of Australia, for contributing to Chapter Eleven. Thanks.

Much gratitude goes to my cover artist, Sarah Jones, for the beautiful water color painting she did of the Sabian Symbol for my Ascendant. Her artistry will further be seen later this year when the 2003 Celestial Influences ® calendar is published.

My dear friend and colleague, Mary Plumb, to you I wish to say Ashland feels like home because of your warm welcome. With my Mars conjunct your South Node, and your Chiron in the degree of my IC, I was your brother the last time around, and I am very grateful to have found you again.

To my new friend, Paula Sendar, who wafted into my life on the sweet breezes of transit Jupiter trine to my Moon and Venus, thank you for being my Valentine.

To my expatriated Portland sister, Laura Tilley, who joined me in Ashland two months after I moved here, thank you, dear, for your love and companionship. It is a comfort to know that you are just across town.

To my friends in the Southern Oregon Chapter of NCGR, Samten Williams, Doug Kellogg and Dana Gerhardt, my appreciation for our astrological community.

To my clients and students who have been with me for all these years, it has been an honor to serve you, and I will continue to do so for many years to come.

To all of the local astrology groups who have invited me to speak in Vancouver, Texas, Phoenix, California, Boston, Connecticut, New York, Florida, Virginia, Philadelphia and elsewhere, thank you for your appreciation of my work.

And, to my big brother, Jim, thanks for always being there. You are the best.

Foreword by Steven Forrest

"Well, Steve, what do you do for a living?"

"I'm a professional astrologer."

Later that evening . . .

"Steve, I know you're interested in astrology, but what do you actually do for a living?"

I've been through that conversation a few dozen times over the past twenty years. People just don't believe you can actually make money as an astrologer. In the popular mind, astrology is a hobby, not a profession. They're wrong! You can prosper reading astrological charts—and it is a profoundly rewarding career in all the ways that count: the work is meaningful, independent, and dignified. It is comfortably remunerative by the standards of most white collar professions. And it is at least slightly cool to boot!

In his third volume of *Astrology: A Language of Life,* which he has subtitled *A Handbook for the Self-Employed Astrologer,* Robert Blaschke charts the course for anyone considering making astrology his or her life work. And he's not just blowing smoke: he's followed that course himself, and wound up prosperous, happy, and respected in his field. Like most of us, he's had defeats as well as victories. He's learned some lessons the hard way. And in the pages that follow he is blessedly forthcoming about everything, from soup to nuts.

We astrologers have created a vibrant renaissance over the past fifty years. We've allowed ourselves to learn from modern psychology, absorbing much of it into our language and practice. We've been thinking deep thoughts about the place of human consciousness in the larger universe. We've ridden the breaking wave of computer technology, and are now armed with a powerful battery of new tools and techniques. We've founded schools, and even opened the soon-to-be-accredited Kepler College of Astrological Arts and Sciences in Seattle. We've held serious conferences with authentic intellectual exchanges and scholarly cross-fertilization. We've become an international community, breaking out of at least some of the insularity of national borders. We've weathered legal challenges and learned how to defend ourselves against anti-astrology witch hunts. We've written a vast library, established serious journals, and compounded data bases for research. As a group, we astrologers are strong, numerous, merrily contentious, and deeply engaged in a profoundly creative process.

Even though astrology is still often treated derisively in the media, our renaissance is spreading through the zeitgeist. Tellingly, a 1977 USA TODAY poll said 17% of Americans "believe in astrology." In 1998, the number was up to 37% That's a more-than-doubled acceptance rate in those twenty-one years—and, from a business perspective, let's add that those numbers represent of lot of potential customers!

I attribute much of the increasing public acceptance of our work to the ongoing efforts of professional astrologers such as Robert Blaschke. They're the ones fighting the trench warfare, winning the hearts and minds of open-minded people one at a time. They have been chipping away at the walls of resistance in the only way that really matters—by supporting real human beings with helpful, accurate astrological perspectives day after day. And those clients have been spreading the word, talking about their positive experiences. In my own practice I've sat with countless people who were "pressured by friends or mates" to see me. Most of them radiated skepticism and doubt upon arriving—and many of them have been back year after year ever since. To me, the battle to restore astrology to its natural place as one of humankind's most precious allies is being won that way, hour by hour and person by person, out there in the real world, by professional astrologers simply doing their work.

There are still too few of us. The field is wide open. The astrological community has been good at education and publishing, but we have been a catastrophe in terms of the practical work of actually helping people give up their "day jobs" and make the switch to full-time astrological work. We've been worse than a catastrophe at getting young people to recognize that astrology is a viable and attractive professional choice. Robert goes straight to the heart of these issues in his practical, Virgo Rising way. I particularly appreciate his Scorpionic willingness to overcome the social taboo about discussing money. That's exactly the kind of practical information that needs to be disseminated if younger folks seeking professional training for their future careers are going to consider the field. We've got to help them break out of this pervasive "astrology-is-a-hobby" mindset. We've got to make the choice "real" in their minds—and money is of course a big part of human reality.

Reading the pages that follow, you'll learn in a step-by-step, nuts and bolts way how to establish and build an astrological practice. Meanwhile, subliminally, you'll get the clear message: *I can do this.* That's a big reason why this book is so precious, and why I am so grateful to Robert for taking the time to share what he has learned.

One last comment. Occasionally, I've had unworthy thoughts about keeping the good news about astrology as a profession under my hat—sort of like not telling anyone about the undiscovered vacation spot you've found. Sometimes I can't believe I actually get paid to do something I love so much. I travel to interesting places, yet I can work at home—no commuting! I've got money in my pocket. My wife and I own a nice house. I don't hate Mondays, at least once the coffee kicks in. I've had a lot of opportunities to hang out with glamorous and influential people. I can dress and look as I please. Getting older only seems to help—no fear about being put out to pasture or "downsized." And, most importantly, I will die knowing that I've made a real difference in people's lives. But whenever I think of keeping the treasure map secret, I just laugh at myself. The potential market for serious astrology is so vast, and the ratio of competent astrologers to potential clients is currently so incredibly lopsided—it feels like a chance to buy stock in Microsoft back in the days when Bill Gates needed to borrow twenty bucks 'til next Tuesday. Why not share it?

Welcome aboard—and, Robert, thanks again for providing this service to us all.

Steven Forrest
31 January 2002
Chapel Hill, North Carolina

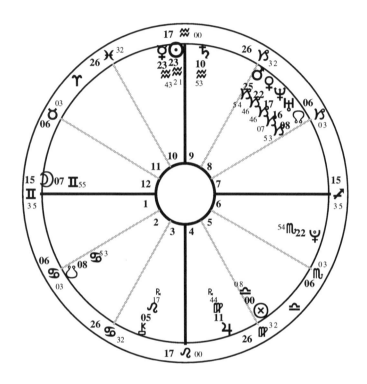

Earthwalk School of Astrology

12 February 1992
12:00 PM PST
Lake Oswego, Oregon
45N14   122W40
Porphyry Houses
True Node

[from business license]

Introduction

During my third Jupiter return at the age of 35, I resigned from my career as an Architectural Hardware Consultant in San Francisco to live my dream of being a full-time professional astrologer. I walked away from a $60,000-a-year financial package which included my salary, a company car, paid gasoline, auto insurance, health insurance, life insurance and a retirement account.

I followed my heart in 1989 to do what I loved full-time, as I knew that being a part-time astrologer could never get me to the depth of astrological knowledge that only full-time immersion would bring. My progressed Midheaven was conjunct my natal eleventh house South Node, my progressed Ascendant was conjunct my natal second house Neptune, and my progressed Mars had just ingressed into his dignity in Scorpio, joining my four natal planets there. Anyone other than an astrologer would have said, "What was he thinking?" Believe me, I have posed that question to myself many times over the last twelve years when I looked in my checkbook and saw only single or double-digit numbers in the balance column.

I have recently reached my fourth Jupiter return at the age of 48, and I have found myself reflecting on the growth and expansion that has come into my life over these last dozen years. I succeeded at my goal to make it as a full-time astrologer, author and lecturer, and I have several hundred regular, loyal and satisfied clients all over the U.S., Canada and abroad. I founded a school of astrology, built an astrological mail-order business, became an astrological software dealer, and started an astrological publishing company and have written three books in a planned series of seven volumes.

Now I feel that I can share my experiences to help other astrologers who are just starting out, trying to make the leap from a part-time to a full-time practice, or attempting to make their existing practice more efficient, better organized and more successful. The intention of this, my third volume in the *Astrology: A Language of Life* series is to produce a practical handbook for the self-employed astrologer that addresses all of their concerns: transitioning from student, establishing a professional practice, handling income, expenses and taxes, marketing and advertising, navigating the client relationship, teaching and local public speaking, writing, publishing and lecture travel, participating in the astrological community, overcoming occupational hazards, and fostering personal/spiritual growth.

I have made many foolish mistakes during the years that I have been a full-time, self-employed professional astrologer. I cannot get those choices back to do over again, but what I can do is share with you my failings so that your business choices as an astrologer might be better informed.

I have also had some success as an astrologer. I want to share these triumphs with you, in the hopes that my work can serve as a pragmatic inspiration to those of you who have similar aspirations and ambitions as I.

These days in the astrological community there are many voices within the national organizations speaking out for education, certification, ethics training and professionalism. There are also two shining examples of astrology's return to the academic world: Kepler College in Seattle, Washington and the Astrological Institute in Scottsdale, Arizona. In addition, The Organization for Professional Astrology has been working hard for years to provide career path assistance and structure for professional astrologers.

Yet, no matter how much astrological education you have received, or how many certification levels you have passed, when you get home from that astrology conference or from that astrological institution, you still have to roll up your sleeves and build your practice one client at a time. It is my wish that this book will stand as a bridge between your education and your practical success.

I am the son of a father with a Ph.D. in Aeronautical Engineering (UCLA; 1953), but I, myself, have no education beyond Saint Monica High School class of 1971. I have set out to prove in my life that hard work, resourcefulness, intelligence and creativity are every bit as valuable as formal education on the road to success and accomplishment. This book reflects my work ethos, and it is the hard working astrologer for whom it has been written.

I have worked for many years carving out a path for myself as a self-employed astrologer, without much knowledge of what other astrologers were doing, how much money they made, and how they ran their practices. I have often perceived a veil of secrecy about this in the astrological community, somewhat similar to how, in polite society, the amount of money one makes is just not discussed. In this book I want to throw a hatchet into the tree of silence, splitting the wood in two so as to allow the inner, hidden creative fire to burn freely.

I am going to tell you exactly how much money I have made as an astrologer, how much my business expenses have been, and how I have earned astrological income. I didn't know what to expect when I was just starting out, and many grey hairs in my beard have come from enduring over twelve years of financial uncertainty.

I believe that astrologers are about to evolve into a greater solidarity with one another as Uranus ingresses into Pisces in 2003. It is my hope that this book will contribute to that process by exposing to the light of day the detailed inner workings of a successful astrological business. *If I can do it, you can do it.* If you are already successfully doing it, I pray that this book will provide a small measure of comfort to you by validating your business model as an astrologer.

It is my sincere wish that the systematic information contained in this book will help you to earn additional money as a professional astrologer by expanding your clientele and by teaching classes locally. It is also my hope that any of you who have the aspiration to write and self-publish your first book will find pragmatic help in this volume to take you closer to your goals.

I wrote this book with my progressed Mercury sextile to my natal Venus, and it has been a labor of love for me. I chose to freely share with you all that I know, and all that I have learned from my experience, in the hopes that you can become successful in your efforts as a self-employed astrologer. We travel the same road.

I also had transit Uranus square to my natal Sun and Mercury while I wrote this book. I started my astrology practice in February 1979 when Uranus stationed on my natal Mercury; the very next year, when Uranus conjoined my Sun three times, I unexpectedly became a father! So, I went back into the corporate world to work for the next nine years, in order to pay child support and maintain insurance for my daughter. Now, one quarter of the Uranus cycle later, I have met every hurdle and obstacle placed in front of me, while attempting to fulfill my life purpose.

I have spoken out forcefully on issues that I have definite opinions about, such as the Internet, professional ethics and astrological organizations. I ask for the reader's clemency with my sometimes radical point of view. My editor implored me to tone down some of the harsher language in the book, but with transit Uranus square my Mercury, I was feeling pretty feisty and ready to tell it like it is.

I started this long and winding road when transit Saturn formed the first of forty-three oppositions to my secondary progressed Moon in August of 1989. As the rulers of my nodal axis, this has kept the pressure on me to succeed, with or without emotional support in my life. I have endured through 25 oppositions, with 18 to go. I'll let you know in February of 2011, when they cease, how I am doing.

I am always available for professional consultation to discuss any of your concerns about marketing your practice, establishing a mail-order business, starting a school of astrology, or getting your publishing company off the ground. We all can learn from each other's triumphs and failures, and mine are always an open book to my fellow self-employed astrologers. Namasté.

Robert P. Blaschke
7 February 2002
Ashland, Oregon

Chapter One

Making the Transition from Student to Professional

To be honest, there is nothing that can quite fully prepare any student to begin practicing astrology. This rite of passage is a patently spiritual leap of faith into an unknowable world that only makes itself visible once the journey has begun. To read the life map of another human soul is a sacred duty; and education, certification and professional preparation are only part of the knowledge needed.

Any practicing astrologer is continually drawing upon his own life experience, and it is a peculiarity of this profession that the subjective wisdom of the consultant is in continual interaction with the objective body of knowledge used. Thus, how the astrologer lives his life and learns from his experiences is perhaps as important as the articulate command of the astrological language and technique.

That said, there is undeniable value in the education, certification, apprenticeship and professional preparation undertaken by students before reading horoscopes for fees. Many astrologers have the unprovable, but obvious recollection of having practiced astrology in past lives, myself included. For us, it is as if we remember astrology, rather than learning it this time around.

Additionally, our profession is filled with self-taught individuals who have never taken a formal course of study in their life, yet have built successful careers as consulting astrologers. They are praised and loved by their clients and students for their knowledge, skill and experience. How can astrology, as a profession, discern which preparatory measures are superior, and which are inferior?

This chapter will summarize the resources available to the student as they ready themselves to undertake a career as a consulting astrologer. I will share my own perspective, including both traditional and unconventional approaches to making the transition from student to professional.

Astrological Education

Just what do you need to know before launching a career as an astrologer? Thirty years ago, when I looked at a horoscope for the first time in this life, it was as important to know how to erect the birthchart manually as it was to be able to interpret it. Computers and astrological software have radically changed not only the practice of astrology, but the education of astrology students as well.

I have taught hundreds of students at my school of astrology, as well as in the bookstores, metaphysical centers, community colleges and other venues where I was invited to teach. My instructional experience has shown me that only about 5% of all of my students have gone on to practice astrology, and only a rare handful have become full-time, self-employed professional astrologers. Who, then, were all of these other students?

I would categorize them as such: a) those with an interest in astrology for self-knowledge; b) those to whom astrology would become a hobby, but not a career; c) those who took a class as a social and intellectual pursuit; d) those who had a general interest in metaphysics or spirituality; and e) those who, once they were exposed to the complexities of this science, declined on further involvement past the rudimentary level.

With these results in my teaching career, I have come to the conclusion that a mentorship/apprenticeship program would ideally be more effective in producing quality astrological consultants for the future of our profession. This option is not yet a practical one, and may never be, as the payment abilities of the student for this type of personal discipleship are as woefully unrealistic as the time commitment, without income, required of the master astrologer.

What we do have available for the education of the astrology student is a fine network of classes and teaching astrologers in just about every city in North America, with the exception of some instructional black holes in the Bible Belt of the Deep South, parts of the Canadian prairie or maritime provinces, and the U.S. Midwest. With the advent of the Internet, and the arrival of astrology schools on-line, astrological education is now available to individuals living in remote and rural areas, as well as abroad in countries with sparse astrological resources.

If you have decided to pursue a career as an astrologer, you have the following excellent choices for formal education: a) Kepler College in Seattle, Washington, is the only college that is authorized to issue BA and MA degrees in Astrological Studies; b) Astrological Institute in Scottsdale, Arizona is a nationally accredited vocational school of astrology with a diploma program; c) ONLINE College of Astrology is an Internet school offering courses for the beginning student through advanced professional levels; and d) a plethora of astrological correspondence courses taught by reputable astrologers worldwide, of which a comprehensive summary was made by *The Mountain Astrologer* magazine in their Feb/Mar 2001 issue #95, and, previously, in their Feb/Mar 1998 issue #77.

Abroad are distinguished astrology schools such as UK's Faculty of Astrological Studies and the London School of Astrology, Achernar in the Netherlands, Astro Logos, Canopus Academy of Astrology and The Chiron Centre in Australia.

On a more informal level, there are teaching astrologers at most metaphysical bookstores. Your local astrological association can also provide you with names of teaching astrologers in your area. Appendix I in the back of this book has contact information for these resources.

Organizational Certification

The National Council for Geocosmic Research (NCGR), one of the four major astrological organizations in the U.S., has built a very impressive educational curriculum over the last twenty years. In addition, NCGR has established four levels of certification, from the basics of chart erection and planetary meanings all the way to the most advanced and complex techniques of rectification. NCGR has biennial education conferences, at which classes on all four curriculum levels are offered, as well as testing for each level.

The International Society for Astrological Research (ISAR), at their Fall 2000 conference in California, presented Certified Astrological Professional (C.A.P.) honors to a group of about 200 astrologers, *grandfathering* them in, based on attendance at an ethics training seminar and minimum of ten years of astrological practice. This C.A.P. program is presently under review to consider tougher standards for qualification.

Predictably, this has caused a squabble between these two organizations. NCGR's point of view, and entirely justifiable, is that educational rigor and testing must be part of any certification process. ISAR is warranted in attempting to move the process of professionalism forward, and introducing ethics training into the mix. Alas, astrological politics! We are no different than the rest of society.

I have a different point of view. As a renegade West Coast intellectual who is not entirely comfortable being part of the astrological establishment, I think that, in some cases, there are astrologers who are better off, and who can make an innovative contribution to our profession, by operating outside of the standards of education and certification. If astrologers are all educated and trained in the same techniques and by the same teachers, where, then, would innovation and original thinking come from?

The American Federation of Astrologers (AFA), another large U.S. organization headquartered in Arizona, also has a substantial educational program and a professional testing criteria. The AFA has many local affiliate groups around the country, and several of its members are seasoned teaching astrologers.

In building my astrology practice over the last twelve years, I have never used any professional or organizational certification to market my consulting or teaching services. Nor have my clients or students ever inquired as to whether I had these credentials. My view is that in the first five minutes of an initial-contact phone call, the client or student hears the love and sincerity in your voice, along with your communication skills and professional demeanor, and makes up their mind as to whether or not they will retain your services.

Mentorship & Apprenticeship

If I lived in a spiritual commune, with a rent-free roof over my head and three square meals a day, I would be more than happy to mentor an apprentice and teach them everything I know about astrological theory and technique. However, all self-employed astrologers are so busy just trying to make a living that it is somewhat impractical to offer mentoring services that would interfere with one's astrological income.

The closest our profession comes to this ideal of apprenticeship is through Internet or mail-order correspondence courses, some offered by the best astrological minds in our professional community. Within these programs personal attention is achieved through the letter, e-mail or telephone interchanges that can take place between student and teacher.

The Association for Astrological Networking (AFAN), the fourth of the major U.S. organizations, has recently implemented a mentor pilot program. Students form a mentor relationship with an AFAN advisor for a period of three months. There is not actual tutoring provided; rather, guidance is available to the student for starting a practice, and one must be an AFAN member to participate.

Testing Your Knowledge Level

One way to prepare yourself to begin your practice of astrology is to test your level of astrological knowledge. This can be accomplished in a variety of ways. One can take an intermediate or advanced class or workshop from a teaching astrologer to see if there are indeed gaps remaining in your astrological skills. Many students who are self-taught, through the reading of astrology books alone, often ask themselves the rhetorical question, 'Do I know enough to interpret birthcharts professionally?'

Another option for measuring your knowledge level is to be tested by an astrological organization such as NCGR or AFA. For example, at each level of certification NCGR has exam preparation help and guidelines for the testing procedure. One can find emotional support here as well as camaraderie with other astrologers who have traveled the same educational road.

Still another option are relationships that can be formed with other astrologers through your local astrological association. Over a beer, or during coffee after an evening lecture, conversations abound regarding techniques used in practice, the challenge of client problems, and the variety of consultation requests that a typical practicing astrologer receives. In this environment, through osmosis, a student of astrology can feel closer to their goal of beginning a practice.

There simply is no substitute for experience. Any professional astrologer, if he is humble enough to admit it, can vividly recall the days early on in his consulting career when he made pages and pages of preparation notes prior to the client arriving for the appointment, only to find that during the consultation less than 10% of his prep work was actually brought up for discussion. This is the dimension of professional astrology that knowledge alone cannot penetrate.

Visiting Another Astrologer to Observe Their Professionalism

In my career, I have had at least 100 other astrologers call me to schedule an appointment for an in-person or telephone consultation. In the majority of cases they were not using my services only to gain perspective about their current transits and progressions, but also to observe my techniques, how I conducted a session, what my fees were, what my office was like, and who I was as a person.

Now, I have four planets in Scorpio, and can usually sniff out any clandestine motives or intentions within the first 30 seconds of dialogue with another human being. So, rather than play a cat and mouse game, I try to put my fellow self-employed astrologers at ease by freely offering to disclose the techniques and methodology I use to arrive at my interpretations.

This is actually an excellent way for an astrology student who is just beginning a practice to observe a professional astrologer within the context of their own birth chart. I am always willing to field questions during a consultation regarding technique, the complexity of multiple planetary influences occurring at the same time, or any other topic that the astrologer/client has queries about.

One instance of this that I clearly recall occurred in October, 1994 when another astrologer, who had just moved to Portland from Maryland, called to schedule a consultation. She told me that my Yellow Page ad looked to be the most business-like and professional amongst all of the astrologers listed, and that she wanted some time with me to see my office, observe my methods and perhaps to contrast her level of astrological skill with mine. She proceeded to build a successful astrology practice for herself in Portland, and I openly shared my entire business model with her in the hopes that it would contribute to her prosperity.

Techniques Required to Start Practicing

I would hate to think that any potential consultant astrologer would delay the start of their professional practice because they felt that they were lacking in technique. My experience is that your command of a variety of techniques arises out of the laws of client supply and demand. You can start your practice with the big three: a) natal interpretation; b) relationship analysis; and c) progressed and transit explication.

As your practice builds you can add the Sabian symbols, esoteric delineation, financial astrology, investment timing, relocational astrology, electional astrology, solar and lunar returns, medical diagnosis, child chart interpretation, vocational guidance, family dynamics, karmic astrology, mundane forecasts, lunar node cycles and eclipse research, and any other techniques required to meet the needs of your clientele.

Natal, relationship analysis and progressed horoscopes will be your bread and butter appointments through the years. Most astrologers will eventually drift into an area of expertise, and actually become known professionally for this method, especially if they publish research papers or write a book about it. I have even had clients ask me if the 'P' in Robert P. Blaschke stood for 'Progressions'!

If you own astrology software, such as Solar Fire, Kepler or Win*Star for Windows, or Io Edition for the Macintosh, you will find every calculation method imaginable. Through your research, using your software's various capabilities with client charts *after* the consultation is over, you will find what you missed in your preparation work and thus be better equipped for your next consultation.

Self-Confidence

If I had to single out the one essential factor for astrology students making the transition to becoming a professional astrologer, self-confidence stands at the top of the list. Your spiritual protection as an astrologer lies in the intention in your heart. If you set this intention as your sincere desire to help others you can never go wrong. Besides, this power of loving service, along with adequate expertise, will fill you with confidence to do the work.

Education, certification, ethics training and professionalism are all good training for the mind. But when you stop to consider that your work as an astrologer is going to have you drawing strength from your heart to consistently come up with the love, compassion and care that counseling requires, what, then, is the training for your heart? Self-confidence, in my view, comes from loving others.

I realize that, with my Virgo rising, my attitude of service is only one of several approaches to practicing astrology. If you are lacking the confidence to begin your astrology practice, I would encourage you to believe in yourself, and then take the best of your Ascendant's qualities and incorporate these virtues into your work.

Doing Mini-Readings at Psychic Fairs

You can also gain confidence as an astrologer, and thus further prepare yourself to begin a professional practice, by getting experience doing mini-readings. Most major cities in North America have one or two metaphysical bookstores, and these businesses often hold monthly Psychic Fairs. Alternative practitioners of all stripes descend on these events, including tarot card readers, palmists, Reiki masters, clairvoyants, numerologists, bead vendors, and the latest in New Age spiritual technology to come down the pike.

You can rent a booth or table space from the organizers at a nominal cost, and sometimes they will take a percentage of your income as well. They sell admission tickets to the general public, and you will find yourself in the midst of a Gypsy bazaar environment. All sorts of colorful characters with head scarves and dramatic costumes from Gothic times provide guidance to the roaming weekend spiritual consumers.

My Capricorn North Node was always mortified when I worked at these fairs. I have dozens of hilarious stories I could tell you about palmists or card readers who sat next to me for ten hours on a Saturday, saying the exact same thing to every $15 client who sat down for a reading. I, myself, without trying to sound too contemptuous here, always tried to represent professional astrology with a modicum of dignity, arriving with my laptop computer, laser printer, power strip, industrial strength extension cord and a sideways look of disdain for the metaphysical riffraff I had to work amongst.

I will give you a tip here on how to pull a natal chart out of the computer printer, or read it from your laptop screen, and always connect immediately with the client during a mini-reading. Take the Lights and the three personal planets, then find any major aspects to Saturn, Uranus, Neptune or Pluto and start talking. You will only have 15-20 minutes to read their horoscope, with no prep time whatsoever, and you will have to learn to be glib, quick and ready to roll. These aspects between the personal planets and the four outer planets will always be central.

Being an In-House Astrologer at a Local Bookstore

Many professionals have paid their dues while they built private practices by working as an in-house astrologer for a bookstore. I have done this myself in the past for a period of time, and I want to discuss the pros and cons with you.

Metaphysical bookstores get a fair amount of retail traffic, and many of them have various practitioners that see clients on the premises. In addition, they often develop a mailing list of customers and send out a periodic newsletter containing a calendar of events and bios on their in-house healers.

There are some plum gigs out there with successful bookstores that have been in business for many years. However, these openings are hard to come by, as they usually already have an astrologer that has been with them for a long time. The business failure rate for small bookstores is pretty high, and has gotten even worse since Amazon.com appeared on the Internet. During the ten years that I had my school of astrology in Portland, I saw several of these stores close down.

If you read about a new bookstore opening locally, you can approach them and offer to provide astrological consultations to their customers. The store will usually have a back room or private office where you can do your work, and the owner or general manager will keep a percentage of your consultation fee. The store usually books the appointment, takes the payment, and then pays you by check. I would advise you to negotiate for a 70%-30% split, with you being paid 70 cents on the dollar.

There are environmental factors that can go negative on you in a bookstore. High noise levels from talking customers and thin walls, or a sound system blasting the latest Enya CD might create an environment where you can hardly hear yourself think, let alone carry on a conversation with a client. I would advise calculating the birth chart on your own computer, even if the store has software to do horoscopes, as I have found repeated mistakes in time-change data entry that resulted in Ascendants being an hour off.

If you can get a position in a bookstore, make sure that you get each client's mailing address and telephone number and start a data base of your own. Then, if the bookstore folds, you can contact the clients and have them come see you in your own office or home.

I will end this chapter with a story for you. I started publishing an Earthwalk Astrology quarterly newsletter in 1992, and regularly and religiously maintained it for many years. It was started out of frustration with the local bookstore where I was the in-house astrologer. I was offering consultations and classes there, and the store was chronically late in getting out their own newsletter which resulted in little time for students to register for my classes.

Transiting Pluto was conjunct my Sun at that time, and I felt a powerful urge well up within me to take control of my own business destiny and just do it myself. I got a bulk-mail permit from the Post Office, put together a data base, learned how to *print-merge* mailing labels, and have been entirely on my own ever since. Best move I ever made. I should mention that the bookstore and I also parted company around this time as well, which was just fine with me as it was the motivational fuel to succeed on my own. Natal Mars in my first house speaking here!

Chapter Two

Establishing Your Professional Practice

In order to take your vision of practicing astrology professionally from an abstract aspiration to a physical reality in the world, you must build a structure to contain it. This form then becomes the vehicle by which your private practice will first establish itself, then grow, diversify and expand, and sustain itself during the years of your career as a consulting astrologer.

Like a child, you should name this entity, nurture it, feed it, protect it and be proud of it. It is your professional offspring, and whatever is done in your name as a consulting astrologer should bear the stamp and seal of your dignity and quality.

This chapter will address the practical dimensions of launching your astrological business. Do not underestimate the significance of even the lowliest tasks that are involved in establishing a professional practice. The importance of creating and maintaining office space, furniture, office supplies, brochures, business cards and the like may appear to pale in comparison to the spiritual importance of reading a life map of another human soul, but you will find that as you organize yourself practically you are sustaining yourself spiritually, for the two go hand-in-hand.

Leasing Commercial Office Space

Step one on the road to creating an astrology practice is to find a habitat for your work out in the world. Astrologers who try to build practices from home offices may not do as well as those who establish a business presence in the community. There are many options available to you for leasing commercial office space.

I have rented many offices in my career, some in professional buildings where I was surrounded by architects, accountants, realtors and insurance agents. I have also leased office space in healing arts centers where I was surrounded by rolfers, massage therapists, Reiki masters, acupuncturists and naturopaths. Additionally, I have rented offices in buildings that predominantly housed psychotherapists and counselors. I even had an office on the Oregon coast where my commercial neighbors were galleries, gift stores and candy shops. I was surprised by what I learned from these experiences.

It is my opinion that an astrologer may actually be happier in a regular office in a standard professional building. In my experience, they have been cleaner, quieter, better-maintained, more professionally run, and were mercifully free of the New Age touchy-feelyness and lack of appropriate boundaries that I encountered at some of the healing centers where I have worked.

Now, I realize that, with my Venus conjunct Saturn, I am not the most huggy kind of guy, except to those that I love and feel affection for. But, that said, I did find it a distraction and a nuisance to walk down the hall coming back from the men's room and feel a subtle obligation to hug every other practitioner in the building with their door open.

To rent commercial office space, you will usually have to sign a lease and procure liability insurance. Lease terms can range from six months to three years, and I have learned that everything is negotiable. The price advertised for monthly office rent is not set in stone. Commercial office space can sit vacant for months, and you, as the lessee, have room to bargain with the lessor. The price is usually set by the square footage of the space, and it is wise to make sure that the owner or property manager pays for the utilities, signage, janitorial services and parking.

To give you a practical overview, I will list the different offices that I have rented over the past ten years, how large they were, how much rent I paid, and the term of the lease agreement:

December 1991	$170/month	150 square feet	6-month lease
June 1992	$178.50/month	same office	lease extension
December 1992	$178.50/month	same office	lease extension
August 1993	$240/month	215 square feet	2-year lease
November 1995	$250/month	140 square feet	1-year lease
November 1996	$350/month	190 square feet	1-year lease
June 1997	$200/month	175 square feet	month to month
May 1998	$350/month	250 square feet	3-year lease
April 1999	$350/month	140 square feet	2-year lease
September 1999	$355/month	195 square feet	1-year lease
January 2001	$275/month	130 square feet	6-month lease

I have had one-room and two-room suites, the latter being the ideal for me as I did my consultations in one office and had my classroom in the other. I have had to break leases when circumstances forced me to move, and I had to forfeit a security deposit in order to do this. I found that building owners and property managers were very fair people, and conducted business in an equitable manner.

One story that I will share with you is *The great eye-watering, sore throat, nasal congestion, new construction chemical blues.* I had watched a new office building under construction in my town for a whole year, a very tasteful development with townhouses, retail space and offices for rent on the upper floor, replete with mountain views.

I knew the owner/developer and used to run into him at the post office a few times a week. He kept after me to break the lease where I was and come be one of his opening tenants. So, after seeing the office just before construction was completed and being seduced by a large window with a view of Mt. Hood, and which also opened for fresh air, I bit and went for it. I found another person to rent my old office (which had no windows), and moved the two blocks to the new one, pushing my desk and other furniture down the sidewalk with a dolly.

Within two hours of moving in, my head felt like I had taken every drug at the pharmacy that produced bad side effects. I was wheezing, my eyes were watering, my throat felt like I had smoked two packs of Camel filterless in an hour, and my nose had this crinkly feeling inside the nostrils. I didn't know what was going on.

Transit Neptune at 4° Aquarius was just coming in to square my natal Venus, and it turned out that I was having an allergic reaction to all the toxic chemicals in the new carpets, sheetrock, paint, and ceiling tiles. My allergies were going bonkers (natal 6th house Moon).

Later that day my first client showed up and said I looked like a cocaine addict, with watering, red eyes, sniffles and a crazed look on my face. Somehow, through the grace of God, I pulled off a great consultation, but as we were finishing I felt on the verge of collapse. She said she was sure it was the carpet fumes and told me about a product called Zeolite that was used in kitty litter boxes to absorb odors.

At this point I was ready to try anything, and she said you could find Zeolite in bulk at natural food stores. So, off I go to People's Food Store, a hippie co-op still around from the late 1960's. I inquired at the check-out stand if they had this stuff. It was way in the back of the store in a rubber tub with a scoop. I put some in a plastic bag and also bought a cloth bag with a string-tie.

Back at my office, I put the Zeolite, which looked like something you would dig out of a dry lake bed, into the cloth bag and then placed it on the floor in a corner. I swear to God I am not making this up, but all the carpet fumes were gone in an hour! That client was my fume-removal angel. Ah, Neptune transits...

Part or Full-Time Aspirations

One important consideration in choosing office space is whether or not you are trying to build a part-time or full-time astrology practice. If you have family responsibilities or other personal limitations that would only allow you to practice part-time, you can find shared office space that you would use two or three days a week, alternating with another practitioner. Professional office buildings that house a lot of psychotherapists would the be the ideal place to look for this type of arrangement.

Many therapists work for county mental health agencies and are slowly building a private practice on the side. They don't use the office full-time and quite often are looking for someone to split the rent. I have even seen offices where four and sometimes five, therapists shared the same space, each coming in one day a week to see their private clients.

It is a spiritual axiom that, unless you know exactly what you want there is no way to obtain it. I always wanted to be a full-time astrologer, and though I had to wait until I was 35 years old to make the change from a part-time astrologer, doing charts on weekends and evenings, to becoming a full-time astrologer, I am grateful for the business experience that I gained in my previous career.

Your Mission Statement & Setting of Intention

When you begin your practice it is crucial to set the intention in your heart as to just why you have chosen to become a professional astrologer. I recommend writing out a mission statement that expresses exactly how you intend to do your work with others. You can be sure that, through the years, your life will have its inevitable ups and downs and you may find yourself reaching in your bottom desk drawer for the wrinkled old piece of paper that had all the idealistic fervor of your beginning days as a career astrologer.

This work is demanding, to be sure, and daily worries can obscure long term perspective. Yet, one's ideals are never destroyed by the vicissitudes of life, only battered and bruised. Creating a mission statement about how you intend to use astrology to help others, along with defining your underlying spiritual philosophy and declaring an intention of loving service to your clients can help you through any of the difficult years of your career.

Electing a Chart for the Start of Your Practice

If there ever were an occasion to elect a chart, it would be for the start of your professional practice. What, you may ask, would constitute the official beginning of your new private practice? Is it when you sign the lease on your new office space? Is it when you move that first piece of furniture through the doorway and place it on the carpet? No. In my view, it starts when you go down to city hall and take out your business license and become an official, taxable commercial entity.

Eight times a year, the Sun sextiles or trines either Mars or Uranus. These are the Cadillac of all aspects for an astrologer to have natally. My recommendation is to pick a day with one of these aspects to elect your chart. Put either the Sun, Mars or Uranus on the Midheaven, but angular in the 10th house and not cadent in the 9th, to time this chart. Make sure that Mercury or Venus are not retrograde, and that the Moon is not void-of-course, but applying to a sextile or trine with a benefic. Ideally, find the time of day when the 7th house ruler is also well aspected to one of the benefics. Tweak the Ascendant to get a positive Sabian Symbol rising, and voilà, you have a chart for your new astrology business!

Office Furniture

To furnish your office you will have to make some practical decisions about the environment you wish to create for yourself and your clients. How much do you want to spend? Should you purchase new or used furnishings? Do you want to go conservative or fancy?

Remember when you watched the evening news and they spoke of the leading economic indicators, and *durable goods* were mentioned? My office furniture is definitely in this category. I still have the wood desk that my former wife gave me for a wedding present in 1983. It has reached its lunar node return, and now I'm going for a second cycle. If you knew how many times I have packed this thing into a 4x8 U-Haul trailer on the back of my 1987 Honda, you would be astonished at how scratch and dent-free it is. Think furniture pads, my friend.

I also have a solid oak computer table that I bought in 1989, with two shelves below for my printer and paper supplies. This is where I write. It is ideal for my iBook laptop, telephone and credit card machine, the three items I use every single working day. I place it at a right angle to my oak desk, and swivel with my desk chair castors between the two.

I also bought my desk chair in 1989, along with my two-drawer filing cabinet. I am telling you the age of my furniture for a specific reason. As you can see, these items are 13 to 19 years old now. When you go shopping for your office furniture you will be tempted to buy some inexpensive stuff at Office Depot or Staples that is constructed of pressboard and fake wood finish. This low cost choice would be a poor investment, as within a year or two the edges will have de-laminated and it will look fairly shabby.

My recommendation is to purchase solid wood furniture, and if you cannot afford a new desk, then buy a used one that is solid wood. It can be cleaned and polished to look like new, and trust me, you'll be happier in the long run.

I have bought two client chairs in my career. I had to buy the second one only because when I was moving my office from Santa Rosa back to the Oregon coast, I ran out of room in the trailer and had to leave it behind. The second one I bought at a used office furniture store for only $50, and is solid oak with dark blue upholstery and in like-new condition.

When I have had couples come for a relationship analysis consultation, I usually borrowed a second chair from the waiting room, not because I was too cheap to buy a second client chair, but because some of my offices were not much bigger than a large closet.

I don't think an astrologer should have a four-drawer file cabinet unless he is a

Cancer or a Taurus and cannot throw anything away. I have several hundred regular clients and have always made do with a two-drawer model. When I get one too many hangnails from trying to cram file folders into tight spots, that is my clue from Spirit that it is time for a Spring cleaning.

I have bought bookshelves from Office Depot, and though they were constructed of the laminated veneer over pressboard, they have held up through the years. The model I recommend is O'Sullivan Industries, Inc. of Lamar, Missouri #61440 Premier Oak. The company makes three different 36" wide bookshelves, with 30", 48" and 72" heights. They even have a toll-free 800 number for getting spare parts.

I have a 30" high bookcase from them, purchased at Office Depot. Other than a slight sag in the removable shelf it has held up quite well. These bookcases will have to be assembled, but if you have Virgo qualities or tendencies like me, and enjoy whipping out your screwdriver, it might actually be fun to assemble.

The only other pieces of furniture I purchased are a client table and a 5' folding table for newsletter production and mailing. I got a 24" x 24" solid oak client table at Cost Plus Imports, manufactured in Singapore, with removable legs that have a bolt, washer, lock-washer and nut assembly to attach them. It has lovely rounded edges, and is quite sturdy and solid, and I only paid about $49 for it in 1989. I place my tape recorder on it during consultations, and the client can put their purse or coffee cup on it during the consultation.

The folding table I got at Office Depot in 1992. It has collapsible legs and a veneer on pressboard surface. This item has been a real workhorse for me. I have set it up countless times at psychic fairs, for doing newsletters in my office, in my classroom for handout collating, and loaning it out at Thanksgiving and Christmas for those large dinner gatherings. With a tablecloth on it, you would never know its humble and lowly mien. These days the 5' folding table sells for $32.99 at Office Depot.

Most commercial office space has neon lighting that is integral with the drop-ceiling construction. I always get spaced out with too much exposure to neon lights. My head starts spinning and I can't think straight. I bought three faux Torchiere floor lamps at a Target store for $19.99 each and put them in the corners with a 100-watt light bulb. It made for a very pleasant and warm environment in which to work. I know Tauruses out there might take offense, but I was on a budget, and these fixtures, with painted aluminum poles and plastic light globes, looked just like Gucci lighting. I never saw a well-heeled client sniff at my lamps.

I am not much of an artsy guy, but nobody wants to work with bare walls, and I have learned how to decorate my offices tastefully and inexpensively. Clients and girlfriends have given me little gifts over the years, like vases, stones, little brass angels and the like, and these sentimental keepsakes I have put on my client table. I have bought Maxfield Parrish posters and a poster of Jesus at the mall, and then got oak picture frames from another store. Using a large paper cutter at a Kinko's copy center, I trimmed the poster to exactly fit the frame. You would never know that I didn't have an interior designer from Beverly Hills do my office.

Computer & Printer

As a self-employed astrologer, your computer will become the central nervous system of your business. You will use it not only for doing horoscope calculations, but also for creating and maintaining your data base and financial spreadsheets, designing business cards, brochures, flyers and magazine ads, for e-mail and Internet access, and for writing your articles, research papers and books.

I would presume that most astrology students these days would already own a computer and printer. If you don't have one, please allow me to make some recommendations for you. I favor a laptop over a desktop computer because of the travel I do as a lecturer, and because it is so compact and takes up so little space. Even though desktop computer monitors are getting flatter and sleeker every year, I suggest that you take a close look at laptops.

I have been a Macintosh user since the 1980's, and presently own a 2001 iBook. My previous computer was a 1993 PowerBook, and I would never have bought a new one for $1299 unless I had to. Sure enough, one day last July, my e-mail stopped working. It turns out that my Internet access provider, Verio, had upgraded their Portland servers from analog to digital, and my internal modem could no longer be authenticated. My choice was to dial-up to an older analog server in Olympia, Washington or in Eugene, both long-distance calls, or get a newer computer. Apple had just come out with these new iBooks, so I went for it.

Man, I went from a 33Mhz processor to a 500 Mhz one, a speed increase of 1500%. It was like Saturn shapeshifting into Uranus. This little baby is lightning quick, and it has the first color screen of my life. Not only that, but my hard drive went from 250 MB to 10 GB, an increase of 40 times! And my RAM went from 14 MB to 64 MB. So, needless to say, making an eight-year technological leap in one fell swoop has been way cool. I have been very pleased with this laptop computer.

I am not the most impartial person when it comes to computer recommendations, and I have very little experience with PC's using Windows. Because I am a dealer for Solar Fire software, and needed to demo the programs, my brother sent me a 1993 Dell 433/L *boat anchor* (his words) with Windows 3.1 installed. It only has a floppy disk drive, and no CD drive, so I am stuck with version 4 of Solar Fire as my limit (version 5 is CD only).

I would recommend a laser printer over an ink-jet printer for several reasons.

Through the years, I first had an Apple ImageWriter. It was so noisy that when I would print a 25-page Natal Interpretation report I would have to put the bloody thing in the closet or go to lunch while it pounded out the report. Next, I got an HP DeskWriter, which was an ink-jet model. Then, in 1993, I bought an HP LaserJet 4ML, which I am still using to this day. It has been like a Buick. You can kick it, drop it, curse at it, and it just keeps on cranking out 4 pages per minute.

I was not happy with the ink-jet printer because it smeared easily. And mailing labels exposed to the rain would run like a woman's mascara when she cries. The replacement ink jet cartridges were expensive and it was pretty slow. I have cranked out thousands and thousands of pages from this LaserJet, as I have had a mail-order business for astrology charts and reports for over 12 years, and it has not been in the shop once.

The replacement toner cartridge only costs $49.99 at Office Depot. I did have to buy an EtherMac iPrint adapter from Farallon to accommodate the new iBook to work with the old serial port on the printer. Realistically, the ability to print color chart wheels with a color ink jet printer does not make up for the smear-free qualities of a laser printer. Black and white is much more practical for your daily business needs such as letters, mailing labels and charts or reports.

Astrology Software

Most students transitioning to a professional practice will already have software to calculate birth charts. If not, this will be a major purchase as you set up your consulting office. The best programs on the market these days sell for about $200-$300. There are programs for calculations only, and then there are report-writer programs that can produce natal, synastry, composite, transit or medical diagnosis interpretations. All of the astrology software manufacturers offer package prices.

I have used the Gamma and Io Editions for Macintosh from Time Cycles Research since the late 1980's to calculate client charts and reports. I also use Solar Fire for Windows to do the more complex calculations such as progressed-to-progressed aspects or transit-to-progressed aspects that the Apple program cannot do. Prior to my Macintosh conversion, my former wife, Stacia, who was also an astrologer, and I had gotten the old Matrix Blue Star program, which ran on DOS, back around 1983. Matrix now makes the popular Win*Star program for Windows.

The Kepler software program comes from Cosmic Patterns, a highly innovative company which has taken my Sabian Aspect Orb technique and created a report in their version 5 that measures the angular separation between planets and then shows the corresponding Sabian Symbol. Cosmic Patterns is also enhancing the forecast programming, which uses techniques outlined in my book on Progressions. The natal aspects are linked to the forming progressed aspects and these, in turn, are linked to transit triggers from the same two planets.

Most of the top programs now have the ACS Atlas included in their price, or for an additional $75 or so. This atlas has all of the time change history for every time zone in the world, along with the latitude and longitude of every city in the world. Before you make your software purchase, be sure that the full atlas is included.

If you intend to do client research as part of your private practice, there are now astrology programs available that can go through all of the calculated charts saved on your hard drive and search for specific criteria. For example, if there is a solar eclipse at 22° Sagittarius coming up, and you wanted to know which of your clients have this degree for their Lights, Ascendant or MC, the Macintosh Io Detective program from Time Cycles Research can hunt through all of your saved charts and make a list of those for whom this degree is prominent.

The AstroDatabank software is another program that has extensive research capabilities. Containing over 20,000 birth records compiled by the astrologer Lois Rodden, this program has 800 organized categories of people, both the famous and the infamous. The software can filter through complex criteria seeking common denominators or planetary signatures.

Word Processing & Data Base Software

To run an efficient astrology practice, you will want to have all of the computer tools necessary to stay organized in your day-to-day business routines. Most new computers now come with pre-loaded software that contains a word processor, data base, spreadsheets, graphic tools, Internet browser and e-mail program. For either the Apple or PC, there will be software such as Apple Works or Microsoft Office included when you purchase your computer.

The astrologer can use a word processor for correspondence, invoices, designing a flyer or brochure, creating a newsletter, or to write articles. These programs now have a spell-check feature and a thesaurus built in, and will help you to send out very professional looking material to your clients.

The core of my astrology business has been my data base. For over ten years now, I have scrupulously and religiously maintained a customer data base. Every client name, address and telephone number, each consultation appointment date, all class or workshop registration, any book sale, tape orders, chart or report purchases, gift certificates bought, astrology calendars, software sales and credit card numbers have been entered into my data base through the years.

From this software I can generate mailing labels sorted by client birthdays, zip codes, or by targeted customer type (i.e. book sales only). A data base is only as good as two key features: a) how many fields you create when you first build your data base, and b) how thoroughly and meticulously you enter the data for each client transaction.

Now, I realize that, with my Virgo rising, I have more patience and aptitude for these kinds of routine business tasks, than, say, the fire signs ascending. I have always been strangely comforted by doing the minor secretarial chores for my practice (natal 6th house Moon), as it helped to balance the deeper spiritual, emotional and intellectual demands of the work.

I will list my 39 data base fields now to help you set up your own.

First Name	Student•Class	Volume I Advance Order
Last Name	Student•Workshop	Volume I Shipped
Address	Tutoring	Volume I Will Call
City	Attended Lecture	Volume I Sold On Tour
State	Software Customer	Volume I Review Copy
Zip Code	Bought Textbook	Volume II Advance Order
Country	Bought Calendar	Volume II Shipped
Phone	Bought Tape	Volume II Will Call
Birthday	Sent Software Flyer	Volume II Sold On Tour
Client Consultation Date	Sent Brochure	Volume II Review Copy
Report Customer	Bought Gift Certificate	Client Notes
Chart Customer	Credit Card #	Referred By
Chart Preferences	Address Change	Colleagues & Vendors

No doubt the Aries risings or Mercuries in Sagittarius are pulling their hair out just now, reacting to the anal quality of this thoroughness. I want to reassure you that if you put this kind of Virgo effort into the creation of your data base, then maintaining it and getting full use out of it will be so much easier.

Business Telephone Line, Voice Mail & Long Distance Service

When you lease your commercial office space, you will need to establish business phone service. This kind of telephone line costs a little more than a residential line, but you will also receive a complimentary listing in your local Yellow Pages by being a business customer. You will additionally receive a listing in the business white pages of your local directory.

If you have a company name other than your name, such as my *Earthwalk School of Astrology*, then make sure you order a second listing so that those customers calling directory information can find you by either name.

Rather than using an answering machine, I would recommend that you pay a little extra and order business voice messaging when you set up your phone service. If you are on the line, or with a client and have the ringer turned off, or out of the office, the incoming call will forward into the voice-mail system and your caller will hear your customized outgoing greeting message. During a consultation, voice mail is less intrusive, as the client won't hear your answering machine turn on.

Where I live in Ashland, Oregon, Qwest is the telephone service provider. I pay $26.40 per month for my business line, and my business voice messaging costs me an additional $15.50 per month. Including taxes and public utility fees, my total monthly business phone cost is about $49. This does not include any long distance.

When you order your phone service, you will have to pick a long distance carrier. Since the deregulation of the telephone companies, this industry has gone bonkers. There is so much competition out there that long distance rates which used to be 25¢ or more per minute are now as low as 5-8¢ per minute.

I use Touch America for my long distance provider. I have instructed Qwest to designate this company for my interLATA calls (long distance calls outside my local calling area), and for my intraLATA calls (long distance calls inside my local calling area). This way I get one monthly bill from the same company. Also, make sure to request a *PIC Freeze* so that no other company can switch your service to them.

You can sign up for a long distance plan that is on a month-to-month basis or on a twelve-month term agreement. You will save about a penny a minute for the term agreement, and your volume of long distance billing will affect the rates they offer you as well. From $0 to $75 a month in long distance billing, you will get one rate, and for either $75 to $250, or $250 and above, you will get further reduced rates. Be careful here, because if you sign a 12-month term plan at a minimum volume per month, and then dip below that, you will still be charged the minimum volume rate.

My small business telephone plan charges me 7.9¢ per minute for interstate calls, 9.5¢ per minute for long distance calls within Oregon, and 17¢ per minute for calls to Canada. I have found that some companies will lower their rates, and not tell you about it, but if you call every six months or so to check and find that there are now lower rates, they will change your account over to the new ones. That reminds me ... I haven't checked my rates since September 1999! Too busy...

Acquiring a Toll-Free Number for Your Clients

As a customer service for your long-distance clients and patrons, I would recommend that you get a toll-free number added to your business long distance account. I have had an 800 number for almost ten years and all of my out-of-state clients use it to call in for their telephone consultations. 60 minutes x 7.9¢ per minute is only $4.74 for an hour phone call. I absorb this added cost as a deductible business expense and it allows my clients to call me worry-free from work, pay phones, friend's houses, or from hotel rooms when they are on the road.

I also use my 800 number when I am on the road lecturing and selling my books. It allows me to check my voice-mail hassle-free from anywhere. My voice-messaging system allows me to press #7 as soon as my outgoing greeting message begins, and then immediately kicks me into the system to retrieve messages.

My children can call Dad on this number, as can my broke friends, (usually other astrologers without enough clientele), or long-distance girlfriends. I can take this 800 number with me whenever and wherever I move. An 800 number belongs to you, and you can have it *ported* to ring in on any phone number that you designate. I have never owned a cell phone, and I have always had just a single business line with the 800 number ringing in on that line.

The interstate or intrastate long distance charges are identical for either out-bound calls that you dial or for in-bound calls on your 800 number. However, my plan charges more for 800 calls coming in from Canada than it does for me to call Canada. So for my clients north of the border, I call them at an appointed time.

Internet Access Account & E-Mail

Over the last several years, my regular telephone communication and standard letter writing has been increasingly replaced by e-mail correspondence. It's fast, it's cheap and it's efficient. Who can argue with a formula like that? Self-employed astrologers are no different than any other kind of small business owner, and can fully benefit from having an e-mail account to communicate with their clients, students and customers.

I have been using e-mail for about eight years now. Although I still prefer the old-fashioned customer service of a telephone call, many of my clients are scheduling appointments, inquiring about appointment availability, and sending follow-up communication after a consultation using e-mail. I also receive orders from the U.S., Canada and abroad for my books, lectures, tapes, and reports. Customers from abroad send credit card numbers, expiration dates and mailing addresses.

My Internet access provider for the last few years, Verio, to whom I was paying $25 per month for an unlimited dial-up account, has just sent a letter informing me that EarthLink will be taking over my account. Verio is getting out of the bottom of the Internet food chain, namely lowly dial-up users such as myself. My monthly charge will actually drop to $21.95 per month for the same type of account.

The bad news, and this has happened to me before, is that I will have to change my e-mail address. As far as I know, the only way to avoid this is to have your own domain name. You can purchase one for about $30 per year from domain registrars like *register.com* or *verisign.com,* and includes one or more e-mail boxes.

With your own domain identity you can receive e-mail through your domain name, which will never change. And when you're ready to set up your own web site you have the domain identity in place. You simply make arrangements to *host* your website pages at an Internet service provider, (which does not have to be the same company that hosts your e-mail service).

Your Internet access dial-up account, along with your web browser software such as Netscape Communicator or Microsoft Internet Explorer, will allow you to use the Internet for purposes other than sending or receiving e-mail. For example, my books are sold through *Amazon.com,* and I can go online and check my sales figures and receive orders at their website.

EarthLink, like Verio once did, or AOL, has local dial-up telephone numbers all over the country, so when I am traveling I can access my e-mail account without a long-distance call from wherever I am. These local dial-up numbers are found, sorted numerically by area code, at the Internet access provider's website.

Office & Postal Supplies

After you lease your commercial office space, get moved in and start to organize your astrology practice, you will need essential office supplies that all self-employed astrologers use on a daily basis. With my Virgo rising, Office Depot is like dying and going to heaven. They have everything you will ever need to run a business, and the lowest prices, too. Staples and Office Max are two other large office supply chains with stores throughout the country.

I shall list everything I have used regularly through the years, in the hopes that it will help you to better organize your office. These products will be used for clients, reports, classes and workshops, mailings and other routine office duties.

Blank Cassette Tapes	Maxell UR 60, 90 and 120 Normal Bias (4, 5 or 6 pack)
Audio Tape Labels	Avery 5198 (12 labels/sheet)
Address Labels	Avery 5160 (30 labels/sheet)
Watermarked Stationery	Southworth P914C (24 lb. Gray/25% Cotton Fiber)
Copy Paper	Xerox 3R5802 (84 Brightness/20lb.)
Sales Order Book	Adams DC4705 (carbonless duplicate/50 sets)
Business Envelopes	Columbian CO125 (4 1/8 x 9 1/2/24 lb./500 box)
Report Covers	Wausau Papers 49521 (110 lb./250 sheet ream)
Report Binding Bars	C-Line 34447 11" x 1/4" White (100 per box)
Tape Mailing Envelopes	Columbian CO955 6" x 9" (28 lb. recycled brown kraft)
Large Clasp Envelopes	Columbian CO990 9" x 12" (28 lb. heavy duty recycled)
File Folders	Smead 153L Letter Size Manila (1/3 Cut Tabs Assorted)
Transparency Film	3M CG5000 8 1/2 x 11 (40 sheet box for laser printers)
Jr. Ruled Legal Pads	Tops 7501 Canary 5" x 8" (12 Pads/50 sheets)
Ruled Legal Pads	Office Depot #305-706 Canary 8 1/2" x 11 3/4" (50 sheet)

Brite Liners	Bic 90326 (6 assorted colors)
Stapler	Swingline 94-02
Travel Stapler	Swingline 85-06
Staples	Swingline S.F.4® Premium #35450 (5000/plastic box)
Heavy Duty Stapler	Swingline 39™ (for astrology report & cover binding)
Heavy Duty Staples	Swingline S.F.® 39™ 1/2" #74711-79392
Mailing Tape	3M Scotch 142 (2" x 800" with 'sure start' dispenser)
Small Bubble Mailers	Jiffylite R#0 (6" x 9")
Medium Bubble Mailers	Jiffylite R#1 (7 1/4" x 11")
Packing Peanuts	Mail Away 00015 (1.5 cubic ft. bag)
Postage Scale	Pelouze P1 (16 oz. capacity x 1/2 oz. increments)
First Class Mail Stamp	Sanford POM® Stamper 00234 (self-inking)
Envelope Flap Wetter	IDL Corporation #27125 (white ceramic)
Business Card File	Newell Office Products (black with clear cover)
Appointment Book	Mead Office Products 70-100-05 Weekly At-A-Glance
Bank Deposit Stamp	OffiStamp "For Deposit Only" (self-inking)
Paper Clips	Acadia No. 1 (100 box)

Think of me while you are walking down the aisle with the *Blaschke shopping list.*

Using the Drawing tool in your pre-loaded computer software such as Apple Works or Microsoft Office, you can create a template page for your consultation tape labels. Using the Avery 5198 sheet of 12 labels, design a tape label similar to mine, shown here. This is a very professional way to send your tapes to clients.

Astrological Consultation

Robert P. Blaschke, Astrologer • 1.800.778.8490

Earthwalk School of Astrology PO Box 832 Ashland OR 97520
Date: Name:

If you invest in astrological report-writing software and are selling reports, you will need to bind them so that they look professionally done. In the above list of office supplies, I detailed two items for these reports: a) Report Covers, and b) Binding Bars, which are thin plastic spines that slide onto the edge of the report to hide the heavy duty staples, as well as covering up the edge of the paper. If you cannot find this C-Line 34447 11" x 1/4" white binding bar locally, you can order it by mail from:

Olympic Office Supply, Inc. 1820 130th Ave. NE Bellevue, WA 98005 425.883.0303

By calling the U.S. Postal Service Priority Mail Supply Center in Indianapolis toll-free at 1.800.610.8734, you can order the following items, free of charge:

Priority Mail Cardboard Envelopes	EP 14G (for mailings under 16 ozs.)
Priority Mail Cardboard Envelopes	EP 14F (2 lb. flat rate regardless of wt.)
Priority Mail Tyvek Envelopes	EP 14

I would advise buying a coil of 100 self-adhesive 23¢ stamps, as this is the current price for each additional ounce over 1 oz. (A consultation tape along with 4-5 printed charts inside a 6x9 envelope weighs about 4 ounces).

Company Name & Logo

As I mentioned at the beginning of this chapter, you will need to build a form and structure for your astrology practice to be contained within, in order for it to grow and prosper. I would recommend that you name your business, rather than have it be just your name alone.

When Earthwalk School of Astrology was established on 12 February 1992 at noon in Lake Oswego, Oregon, my astrology practice was forever transformed. No longer was it just me as a full-time astrologer. Now I had a business with a separate name and identity. Legally and financially I was still a sole-proprietor, but energetically everything changed.

There was a Sun-Mercury conjunction at 23° Aquarius exactly conjunct my natal Vesta, and square to Pluto at 22° Scorpio, which was conjunct my natal Sun. The Moon at 7° Gemini was conjunct my natal Part of Fortune, and the Earthwalk nodal axis at 8° Cancer-Capricorn T-squared my natal Mars at 8° Libra. Earthwalk's Mars, at 25° Capricorn, is conjunct my natal North Node. The Part of Fortune at 0° Libra is on the Cardinal Point. My company was founded at the applying Uranus-Neptune conjunction, while I have the waning square natally.

Your astrology business will take on a character of its own. While it most certainly reflects you and your love for astrology, it, too, has a distinct life force. I would recommend hiring a graphic artist to design a logo for your company, as this formalizes your business entity into a visual reality beyond just the name.

In 1993 my graphic artist presented me with three different conceptual sketches for a logo and I chose the one shown below. The cost was $275. Once completed, I had it scanned and saved as a PICT file for use in brochures, business cards, flyers, newsletters and display ads.

I am now known as much by being Mr. Earthwalk as I am by being Robert. My company has grown from being a school, mail-order business and an astrology software dealership into a publishing company. A logo symbolizes the essence of a business, ideally as does the company name. Every time I pick up the phone and say *Earthwalk Astrology,* I am representing something greater than myself.

Brochures & Letterhead Stationery

Later in this book, in Chapter Four on Marketing & Advertising, I will discuss ways to promote your practice and astrology business. Two of the things you will want to accomplish as soon as you begin your private practice, are to design a professional brochure and create a letterhead for your correspondence.

Office Depot carries 28 lb. trifold brochure paper stock which is scored twice for folding the 8 1/2" x 11" sheet into a three-panel brochure. The company in Canada that makes this trifold brochure paper is *Domtar,* and you can find them online at *www.domtar.com* or call them toll-free at 1.888.267.1567 to see where their products are available locally.

You can go into your drawing tool software and choose horizontal orientation in Page Setup, and then create three vertical panels measuring 3.5" x 8.5" along with two gutters of 0.25" width each. This layout will fit into the trifold brochure paper precisely. You can create one brochure template for the inside panels and a second for the outer three panels. In the middle panel of the outer three, rotate the text box 90° and put your return address in the upper left hand corner. Now your trifold brochure can be used as a mailer by just adding a stamp and an address. Then run the brochure paper through your laser printer twice to print both sides.

I used to spend several hundred dollars at a time having a printer make brochures, business cards and letterhead stationery for my astrology business. Now I make them all myself on my computer, then buy the appropriate paper stock at Office Depot, and print just as many as I need on my laser printer. The output looks just as professionally done, and the cost savings are substantial.

For sending out your mailing correspondence with a professional look, you can buy a box of 25% Cotton Fiber watermarked 24 lb. stationery paper. Office Depot carries an 80-sheet box made by the Southworth Company, #P914C. Choose a new

Word Processing document in your software program, then choose center alignment and create a letterhead template for your business. Mine looks like this:

Robert P. Blaschke, Astrologer
Earthwalk School of Astrology Publishing
PO Box 832 Ashland OR 97520 USA
541.488.7462 • 1.800.778.8490
ewastro@earthlink.net

Letters that you send out with a letterhead like this will look and feel just like professionally printed stationery, but at a fraction of the cost.

Business Cards

You can also save money on printing costs by making your own business cards. Office Depot carries 65 lb. business card paper stock that has ten perforated cards on one page. One company that makes these is *Geographics.* A package of 25 sheets makes 250 business cards. There are a variety of designs and colors available (I use their 'Impressionistic' design). *Geographics* can be reached at 1.800.426.5923 to find where their products are available locally.

Granted, these will be a bit flimsier than the business cards that you would get professionally printed on heavier card stock, but they are certainly adequate and nothing to be ashamed of. My do-it-yourself 2" x 3.5" business cards look like this:

Robert P. Blaschke, Astrologer
Earthwalk School of Astrology

541.488.7462 • 1.800.778.8490
PO Box 832 Ashland OR 97520 • ewastro@earthlink.net
Author: *Astrology: A Language of Life*
Volume I - Progressions • Volume II - Sabian Aspect Orbs
Volume III - A Handbook for the Self-Employed Astrologer
Faculty member: ONLINE College of Astrology
http://www.astrocollege.com/admin/courses/blaschke.html

On the back of the business card paper package you will find instructions on how to create a template page in your computer software. Top and bottom margins, along with left and right margin dimensions are listed. Some of the newer software programs even have templates built in for *Avery Business Cards* #8371 or #5371, which are the same size as the *Geographics* layout.

Sole-Proprietorship Business License

When you start your private practice as a self-employed astrologer, you are, in essence, creating a legal entity that is subject to taxation and licensure. Most astrologers fall into the category of a *sole-proprietorship*. This means that you are an individual small business owner with no employees.

There are city, county and state government agencies that regulate and tax small businesses. When you begin your private practice, you will have some choices to make that will affect your future as an astrologer. You might think that you can work from a home office, get paid in cash under the table, and declare no consultation income to be taxed. This is the last thing that you want to do.

If you do this, your practice simply will not grow. There are metaphysical laws, not to mention earthly laws, which govern the individual's relationship to his community. Declaring your business to be in existence, subject to licensure and taxation, is the only way that you can grow an astrology practice into a thriving and prospering business entity.

It is a very simple procedure to obtain your business license. This process varies from state to state, and cities and counties will have differing requirements, but the gist of it is the same. The place to start is to call your local city hall, and ask for the *Business License Information* department. This phone number can be found in the Government pages of your telephone directory. This municipal office will be able to tell you if a county and/or state license is required as well, and will also provide you with the phone numbers for these agencies.

If you name your astrology business other than your name (i.e. Earthwalk School of Astrology), then you will also need to register this name with the State or County in which you are doing business. For example, in Oregon this means registering the company name with the Secretary of State's Corporation Division Business Registry Office.

In California, on the other hand, you will have to file your company name with the Office of the County Clerk, and then place a *Fictitious Business Name Statement* in a local newspaper for four issues. You now become a *DBA*, which means that Robert P. Blaschke is *doing business as* Earthwalk School of Astrology.

I have practiced astrology professionally since 1979 in the states of California, Washington, Hawaii, Maine, Oregon and South Carolina. To give you a practical overview of the cost of various licenses, the following is a sampling of mine:

City of Lake Oswego, Oregon	1992	$90 per year (renewal was $60/yr.)
State of Oregon	1992	$12 register assumed business name

City of Beaufort, South Carolina	1995	$32 per year
City of Bellevue, Washington	1996	$21 per year
City of Cannon Beach, Oregon	1997	$104 per year
County of Sonoma, California	1997	$26 filing fee
City of Portland, Oregon	2000	$100 per year

Liability Insurance

Most leases for commercial office space will require you to procure liability insurance. These policies exist to protect the building owner, and you as his tenant, from being sued by one of your clients should they trip on the entry steps, slip and hurt themselves in the parking lot, or walk through a plate glass window.

I have had a business policy with State Farm Insurance for many years, and the annual premium has never been higher than $175. This policy covered me for $2 million in business liability, $5000 in medical payments, and for $11,000 in building personal property (money to replace my losses in a fire). Additionally, this policy covers *loss of income* should the building become uninhabitable.

I also carry an *Inland Marine* policy with State Farm Insurance. This is a policy that covers my laptop computer and laser printer while I'm traveling. The premium is only $50 per year, and gives me $3,000 in replacement coverage for these items.

Post Office Box & Bulk-Mail Permit

As you can tell from this chapter, I have been somewhat of an itinerant astrologer during my career. I had several married years when I was settled, then nearly capsized while my personal life was turbulent, finally getting my leaking boat seaworthy again after the dark night of the soul. I have no planets in earth, so, when life throws me a curve ball it takes me a long time to recover and restabilize.

I am telling you my tales of woe for a purpose. The two things that have remained relatively unchanged for me, despite all of my mutations, have been a toll-free 800 number for my clients and my mailing address. As you start your private practice, I recommend that you get a post office box for your business address.

There are several reasons for this. Firstly, it allows you to get your mail at any time of day or night (most post office lobbies are open 24-7). Secondly, it will protect your privacy, should you wish not to make public your office location. Thirdly, it separates your business from your home life. And, lastly, it creates a stable business address that will not change should you move across town.

In Ashland, I pay $27.50 semiannually for a small (size 1) post office box. There is also a $1 refundable key deposit. Larger boxes cost more, and smaller town rates can be less than the bigger cities. Some post offices have combination locks on the boxes, but nowadays most have key locks. If you receive a package that is too large to fit in the box, it will either be placed in a locker and a key will be left in your box to retrieve it, or a notice slip will be left and you will have to claim it.

Many self-employed astrologers send out newsletters to their clients and students. These mailings are usually bi-monthly or quarterly. If you develop a mailing list with over 200 names and addresses, you can find substantial postage savings by using *standard mail* in lieu of *first class mail* (formerly known as *bulk mail*).

In order to qualify for *standard mail* rates, you will have to get a permit which costs $125 per year. Additionally, in order not to have to use stamps on these mail pieces, you have to pay a one-time application fee of $125 for a *permit imprint*, which allows you to print the following on the upper right hand corner of the outside of your newsletter:

> **Presorted Standard**
> **US Postage Paid**
> **Portland OR**
> **Permit No. 247**

To give you an idea of the postage savings, first class mail presently costs 34¢ for the first ounce, and an additional 23¢ for each extra ounce. The most that you pay for standard mail, for a letter than can weigh up to 3.3 ounces, is currently 25.3¢. This rate is lower (23.3¢) if you can presort your mailing by zip code with more than 150 pieces going to a single 5-digit zip code, or to a 3-digit zip code area. If you can produce bar-coded mailing labels, you then qualify for an even lower *automation* rate which can be as little as 15.3¢ to 17.7¢ per mail piece.

In Chapter Four, I will further discuss newsletters and bulk-mailings as a means of marketing your astrology business. My mailing list has gotten as high as 2,300 addresses, and I have presently pruned it to about 1000 clients, students and book, tape or report customers. I have also *piggybacked* conference information for UAC and ISAR events by including brochures inside a mailing, as the 3.3 ounce limit allowed for a heavier piece to be sent at no additional cost.

Astrological Mail-Order Business for Charts & Reports

All self-employed astrologers find out in a hurry how erratic clientele income can be. Even after being a full-time astrologer for 13 years, I have a variation of scheduled consultations numbering between 15-30 appointments per month. As a result, most astrologers, out of necessity, have to create other revenue streams in their business to stabilize their monthly income.

In establishing your astrology practice, it would be wise to immediately create a mail-order business for computer charts and reports. I have been doing this since

1989, and it has been a most helpful source of extra income in addition to my consultation earnings through the years.

If you have invested in report-writing software that produces natal, synastry, composite or transit interpretations, these reports can be sold for about $25 each, and shipping charges can be added to each order. I offer a quantity discount for orders of more than one report, with two selling for $47.50, three for $67.50, four for $85, five for $100 and six for $112.50.

I would recommend that you ship these via Priority Mail. Cardboard envelopes are available at no charge, and these mailings can get across country in 2-3 days. Earlier in this chapter, you will find the toll-free number to order these envelopes. You can also get them at your local post office.

I also sell computer charts for $5 each when one or two are ordered, and $4 each for three or more. I add a $1 postage fee to orders of three or more charts. I also fax charts to some of my customers, and I receive orders over the phone by credit card for these services. At the peak of my marketing of this part of my business, I earned $10,743 during 1995 selling charts and reports.

Becoming an Astrological Software Dealer

One other source of income for the self-employed astrologer is through selling astrology software and receiving a commission. After you begin your professional practice, open an office and start your mail-order business for charts and reports, I would recommend that you contact various astrology software manufacturers and offer to be a dealer for them in your local area.

Astrolabe, Cosmic Patterns, Matrix, Time Cycles Research and other companies making astrology software need local astrologers such as yourself to demo and sell their programs in your city. You will be paid a 40% commission for these sales. If you sell a retail $295 program, your dealer cost would be $177 and your gross profit is $118. The company will also provide you with catalogues, flyers and other sales tools.

If you are both a consulting and teaching astrologer, you will have students who will be shopping for their first astrology program. As a professional astrologer, you are in the ideal position to make recommendations and sell this software.

I am a dealer for Time Cycles Research, selling their Io Series Macintosh programs since 1991. I have also been a dealer for Astrolabe since 1998, selling Solar Fire programs for Windows. During my best years for sales of software, I sold $8772 worth of programs during 1996, $6932 in 1994, $6547 in 1995 and $6307 in 1999.

The astrology software companies can be reached at these phone numbers:

Astrolabe; Brewster MA	508.896.5081	Solar Fire
Cosmic Patterns; Gainesville FL	352.373.1504	Kepler
Matrix Software; Big Rapids MI	231.796.6343	Win*Star
Halloran Software; Los Angeles CA	818.901.1221	AstrolDeluxe
AIR Software; West Hartford CT	860.232.6521	Star Trax
Time Cycles Research; Waterford CT	860.444.6641	Io Series
AstroGraph Software; Santa Cruz CA	831.425.3686	Time Passages

Chapter Three

Handling Income, Expenses & Taxes

Becoming a self-employed astrologer with no other sources of income, nor a spouse to help pay the bills, can be a requisite journey for idealists, fools and visionaries blinded by a romantic calling. With a 2nd house Neptune, and Venus in detriment, you are probably thinking "this is the last guy I should get financial advice from" about an astrology business. Well, I also have the ruler, Venus, accidentally dignified and conjunct Saturn in that second house, and I have endured many years of financial hardship because I believed in myself and in my eventual success.

Over the last thirteen years, I have been through it all, my friend. I have been down to four bucks left in my checking account, the MasterCard at its limit, and no money for groceries until a client's check showed up in the mail. I have been on my knees and praying for a miracle. I have seen how the spiritual laws of effort and grace manifest, and I have had $500 show up in my post office box on the last day of the month over and over again, just when I thought I was toast.

I have also been flush with nine grand in my business checking account, coming home after a series of lecture and book-signing trips where I earned some decent money in a short period of time. I have been able to write a check for $1299 to buy a new laptop computer without flinching, and I wrote a check for $3644 to pay the printer for Volume II's second press run without batting an eye.

I love astrology. Because of that simple fact, I, under my own Uranian free will, took the road less traveled at the age of 35, for, in my soul, I had to. I walked away from a secure job with all of the benefits, the insurance, and the certainty. It is precisely because of my second-house Neptune that I always believed that I could make a living doing the spiritual work of a professional astrologer.

In this chapter, I am going to tell you exactly how much money I have made as an astrologer over the years, how much my expenses have been running, and how I have made money as a self-employed astrologer. I will confess to my Jupiterian blunders and excesses, where I have spent tons of money on advertising and other expenses that produced no appreciable results.

I didn't know what to expect when I was just starting out, and back then I would idly count the number of clients that I postulated I could see in a day, and then multiplied that times how much I was going to charge for a consultation ($65 back in 1989). I truly believed that I would be earning that much money in no time at all, and here it is 13 years later and it has never worked out that way!

Astrologers don't talk much about what they earn, at least not openly. As I mentioned in the Introduction, I want to change that in this book and bust open some taboos. I was told in 1971 while traveling across country that locksmiths, cab drivers and astrologers are the biggest windbags in the known world. I have been all three of these in my life, and, while I am not sure what that says about me as a person, I think that being Mercury-ruled has something to do with it.

I have been dead broke, but when a client would call for a consultation, I would not schedule it until the following week, too proud to let on that my appointment book looked like the Gobi desert. I don't know if any of my readers have ever done this too, but it is my hope that students transitioning to a professional practice see in this chapter the reality about what it has actually been like for me financially, and that my story might ease their ways.

Categories of Astrological Income & Expenses

Very few astrologers make a lot of money. Most of us are just regular middle class people working within a profession that is not viewed as one by mainstream society. There is a short list of astrologers who make six figures or more per year. These fortunate souls are either syndicated columnists, successful financial astrologers with corporate clientele, software company owners who have been programming since the 1970's, Internet pioneers who got there first in 1995 and built successful websites, or the handful of famous authors amongst us who consult with the affluent for substantial professional fees.

The rest of us are the backbone of the profession. I have earned money in a variety of ways as an astrologer. I realize that, with my Gemini Midheaven, this business model may not be for everyone, but I want to share it with you so that you can see the range of potential income sources for an astrologer. My practice has evolved, grown and diversified, expanding into a mail-order business, school, software dealership, author and lecturer, publishing company, and Internet teaching.

There is a logical sequence involved in assembling a successful astrology career. One must start locally, building a clientele, teaching and speaking publicly in your city, then expanding one's range of products and services. Next comes writing, and becoming known regionally, nationally and internationally. There are income opportunities for self-employed astrologers at each step along the way.

Individuals who own a business quickly learn about the difference between gross income and net income, and how to keep expenses under control so that the net gradually becomes a higher percentage of your gross. Certain ways that you make money as an astrologer will change over the years, and your willingness to let go of non-profitable areas of your overall business is essential in having income increases in other categories.

My present classifications of astrological gross income are eightfold:

    1) Personal consultations   2) Software sales

    3) Book sales   4) Chart & report sales

    5) Online college teaching   6) Writing for websites

    7) Tape sales   8) Speaking fees

To show a sample percentage of my overall gross that each of these categories were, I will give you the breakdown of my 1999 earnings, when I grossed $49,086:

1) Clients	$16,108	32.82%
2) Software	$6,307	12.85%
3) Books	$10,214	20.81%
4) Charts/reports	$4,888	09.96%
5) Classes	$3,024	06.16%
6) Workshops	$2,065	04.21%
7) Tapes	$3,712	07.56%
8) Speaking	$2,768	05.64%
	$49,086	100.01%

To illustrate how categories of astrology income can change over the years, the following is the breakdown of my 1994 earnings, when I grossed $37,366:

1) Clients	$13,627	36.47%
2) Software	$6,932	18.55%
3) Books	$919	02.46%
4) Charts/reports	$10,146	27.15%
5) Classes	$3861	10.33%
6) Workshops	$1670	04.47%
7) Writing	$100	00.27%
8) Speaking	$111	00.30%
	$37,366	100.00%

As you can see, after I became an author and started my publishing company, book sales increased to 1/5 of my gross in 1999. During 1994, prior to when I was an author, and only selling textbooks to students at my school, book sales were only a minimal percentage of my income. Tape sales were non-existent for me in 1994, but by 1999, had become a solid part of my mail-order business. Computer charts and reports, which I used to market more aggressively, were over 1/4 of my gross in 1994, but by 1999, had dropped to less than 10%.

The general rule of thumb is that, early on in your career, other than consultation income, a sizeable percentage of your earnings will be from other astrologer's work; i.e. selling computer reports, software or books written by others. Then, your income will evolve more and more from your creative work; i.e. your book and tape sales along with lecturing income.

My 2001 gross income was $48,219, and fell into the following percentages:

1) Clients	$23,148	48.01%
2) Software	$1,267	02.63%
3) Books	$13,582	28.17%
4) Charts/reports	$1,120	02.32%
5) Teaching	$1,459	03.03%
6) Writing for websites	$200	00.41%
7) Tapes	$2,844	05.90%
8) Speaking	$4,599	09.54%
	$48,219	100.01%

This past year, clients, book sales, tape sales and speaking fees amounted to over 91% of my gross income as an astrologer. It was initially hard for me to let go of some of the bread and butter income from my earlier years, such as chart sales, report sales and class/workshop tuition.

But, natural laws are at work in any business. For the astrologer to succeed long term, he must be willing to beget new sources of income through his own creative work and let the other income sources go. I have also experienced more fulfillment in earning money through my artistic endeavors, such as writing and lecturing.

When you begin your private practice, you will incur business expenses in a variety of categories. My index of expense classifications looks like this:

1) Office rent	2) Phone service/long distance
3) Insurance	4) Postage
5) Copies	6) Office supplies
7) Advertising	8) Books (wholesale cost/printer's cost)
9) Memberships	10) Conferences
11) Licenses	12) Software (wholesale cost)
13) Lodging	14) Meals
15) Miscellaneous (Internet access, bank card discount, bank fees, etc.)	

It is essential for the self-employed astrologer to keep track of all expenses. You only have to pay taxes on your net income, not on your gross. And until you get organized with record-keeping of business expenses, you will not create a smooth-running practice. It is far better to start off on day one putting effort into income and expense records than to play catch up when you get an IRS audit, or are filling out year-end questionnaires for your tax consultant.

The following is the expense percentage breakdown of my practice during 1999:

1) Office rent	$4,200	14.96%
2) Phone/long distance	$3,432	12.22%
3) Insurance	$182	00.65%
4) Postage	$4,616	16.44%
5) Copies	$56	00.20%
6) Office supplies	$2,652	09.45%
7) Advertising	$2,956	10.53%
8) Books	$1,752	06.24%
9) Memberships	$135	00.48%
10) Conferences	$380	01.35%
11) Licenses	$100	00.36%
12) Software	$4,076	14.52%
13) Lodging	$72	00.26%
14) Meals	$246	00.88%
15) Miscellaneous	<u>$3,221</u>	<u>11.47%</u>
	$28,076	100.01%

[Bankcard discount = $843; Merchant services terminal rental = $288; Bank charges = $117; Check printing = $42; Tax preparation = $170; Internet access = $245; Moving expenses = $17; Tuition refund = $170; Bankcard assessment = $78; Imprinter rental = $5; Parking = $44; Client change = $41; UPS = $78; Magazines = $4; Airfare = $600; NSF check = $28; Charitable contribution = $15; Rental car gas = $92; Turnpike = $9; Rental car = $288; Foreign exchange = $7; Limo = $40; Total miscellaneous = $3221]

Subtracting 1999 expenses of $28,076 from 1999 gross earnings of $49,086 gave me a net income of $21,010 for the year. This monthly average of $1751 was the net income from which I paid taxes, housing costs, groceries, utilities, etc. The net income that I actually paid taxes on involved more complex math than this. Unsold inventory, in addition to *cost of goods sold*, were factored in. Later in this chapter, I advise getting help with taxes. Taxes are not deductible as expenses.

What could I have done during 1999 to reduce my expenses and help my business achieve a higher net income? In retrospect, a large marketing effort for *Volume I* that only broke even was a questionable decision. I purchased a mailing list from another astrological business, and sent out a 3000-piece bulk mailing. The postage cost $707, the paper and copying costs were $180, and I paid $230 for the mailing list. With this total cost of $1117, I needed to sell 115 books to break even. I sold about 120. As you can tell, gross income is not net income!

If you attended business school, you would learn about operating budgets, and what percentage each category of expense should be in a profitable small business. For example, a marketing budget should not surpass 6-7% of total gross revenues per year. But, a start-up company may exceed that for the first few years, and then level off at that number later on down the road.

Self-employed astrologers are no different than any other business when it comes to tracking income and expenses. An astrologer just starting out may spend more on advertising during his first years in practice. Later, when his repeat clientele and referral network matures, those advertising costs could then be reduced.

Creating Spreadsheets to Organize Your Practice Financially

As I mentioned in Chapter Two, all new computers these days include pre-loaded software such as Microsoft Office or Apple Works. Spreadsheets are an integral part of these programs, and can be used to organize your practice financially.

Spreadsheets consist of vertical columns that are named for different categories of income or expense, and of horizontal rows which you name for each month. These programs have built-in adding and subtracting engines, and are quite simple to use after they have been set up. Just like your database, a spreadsheet is only as good as how well you maintain it. Sample rows and columns would look like this:

	CLIENTS	SOFTWARE	BOOKS
January	$1697.50	$0.00	$1114.08
February	$1408.95	$493.00	$1111.91
March	$1661.00	$1249.50	$685.74
April	$1760.75	$1114.00	$612.76
May	$1235.00	$366.00	$967.65
June	$900.75	$313.00	$1257.90
July	$1230.85	$0.00	$826.53
August	$1161.75	$509.50	$826.41
September	$1193.75	$698.50	$516.32
October	$1617.50	$0.00	$1363.46
November	$1049.50	$678.50	$703.81
December	$1190.40	$884.50	$227.18
Yearly Totals	**$16107.70**	**$6306.50**	**$10213.75**
	CLIENTS	**SOFTWARE**	**BOOKS**

These spreadsheet figures are from my 1999 gross income as shown on page 37. A program such as this, as you make a monthly entry, will automatically add the income category vertical column to give you an ongoing year-to-date subtotal. The program will also add the horizontal rows to give you a monthly income total.

You will want to design a form with your computer on which you can itemize each bank deposit that you make. Separate out cash from checks, and identify the deposited money as to which classification of astrological income it came from; i.e. clients, reports, books, etc. I fill in this form manually by pencil at each deposit throughout the month; then, at month's end, I add up my income categories and enter these totals into my computer spreadsheet.

Similarly, you will also want to design a form on which you itemize all of your monthly business expenses. I first created file folders entitled *Office Supplies, Copies, Advertising, Lodging,* etc., and in these folders I put my receipts for each purchase or expense. At month's end I total each expense category and enter the figures in my expense spreadsheet, which looks like this:

	RENT	PHONE	INSURANCE
January	$350.00	$0.00	$0.00
February	$350.00	$397.24	$0.00
March	$350.00	$276.32	$0.00
April	$350.00	$460.46	$0.00
May	$350.00	$0.00	$0.00
June	$350.00	$261.00	$181.65
July	$350.00	$531.48	$0.00
August	$350.00	$110.34	$0.00
September	$350.00	$335.21	$0.00
October	$350.00	$323.41	$0.00
November	$350.00	$330.60	$0.00
December	$350.00	$406.02	$0.00
Yearly Totals	**$4200.00**	**$3432.08**	**$181.65**
	RENT	**PHONE**	**INSURANCE**

By creating spreadsheets for both your astrological income and expenses, you will better organize the financial aspect of your practice, and streamline the process for your bank deposits, filing of receipts, and organization for taxes.

Paying Estimated Quarterly Taxes

The self-employed astrologer, usually classified as a *sole proprietorship* for tax and regulatory purposes, is required to pay estimated quarterly taxes. These taxes are due on the 15th of January, April, June and September, or, if these dates fall on a weekend, on the next business weekday.

My astute readers will notice that there is a two-month period of time between your April and June payments, whereas there is a four-month gap between September and your 4th quarter payment due in January. Self-employment tax, in addition to federal tax, is part of this requirement, because the astrologer has no payroll deduction for Social Security taxes.

The Internal Revenue Service, a division of the U.S. Department of the Treasury, has a payment voucher form, 1040-ES (OCR), that must accompany your check, which is made out to *United States Treasury*. These payments must be postmarked by the due dates in order to avoid late penalty fees.

The majority of states in the U.S. have a state income tax that must be paid on these same quarterly dates. The following states do not have a state income tax:

1) Alaska   2) Florida   3) Nevada   4) South Dakota
5) Texas   6) Washington   7) Wyoming

Two other states, New Hampshire and Tennessee, limit their state income tax to dividends and interest income only, so the average astrologer will not pay taxes in these two states The tax rates vary from state to state, and, in some cases, the rate is a percentage of your federal tax liability.

Early in my career, in order to arrive at estimated quarterly tax payment amounts, I calculated complex mathematical formulas based on *annualized gross income* for the whole year (e.g. in figuring my June payment, I would take my January through May gross income, divide it by 5, and then multiply it by 12 to get a yearly estimate).

Then, I would subtract my year-to-date expenses to get my net income up until that month. Next, I would find out what my expected tax would be for the whole year based on my projected *annualized net income.*

After subtracting 1/2 of my self-employment tax (15% of net) from this figure, I got my *adjusted gross income.* Then, I would subtract my standard deduction and one exemption and arrive at my *taxable income.* Most astrologers will have a 15% federal tax rate, and to that I added my 15% self-employment tax. This sum was my projected *tax owed* for the entire year.

From here, I subtracted any estimated quarterly payments made earlier in the year, then divided the remainder by the number of payments left in the year, and voilà, I had my federal amount to pay. You probably don't want or need to hear about the remaining math to be done to arrive at the Oregon state tax amount!

If your head is spinning now, believe me, so was mine as I did these computations. I used to go drink a beer or two after I dropped the damn envelope in the mail. With my Virgo rising and retrograde Mercury in Scorpio, I have commonly done things either backwards or with much more complexity than was really necessary.

Using the Services of a Licensed Tax Consultant

Finally, after being in business for several years, I was guided to the tax angel: Marlene MacEwan, a Licensed Tax Consultant. When I lived in Lake Oswego I used to walk by her office everyday. One fine morning she must have dropped some stardust out the window, because I instinctively just walked into her office building and got in the elevator and arrived at her door.

She laughed out loud as I explained my quarterly mathematical gyrations, and, with tears of mirth running down her cheeks, she said, "just pay 5% of your gross to the feds and 1% of your gross to the state." It was one of those peak moments in life, like good sex or good wine, or both, when you had this Aha! realization. I left her office, skipping down the sidewalk, whistling my way back to work. You know the joke about Scorpios and taxes...

Over the last several years, Marlene's tax advice has been right on the nose. Now, when I am paying my estimated quarterly taxes, I just multiply the gross income for that two, three or four month period by .05 to arrive at my federal payment, and the gross by .01 to get my state tax amount. Each April, when she does my yearly taxes, I have paid almost exactly the figure due through my estimated quarterlies.

I pay a professional fee of $170-$200 each year for her to do my tax preparation. Believe me, she is worth every penny. As my business diversified, (for instance, I now have unsold inventory as a publisher), her expertise puts my mind at ease. I would encourage all self-employed astrologers to use a licensed tax consultant.

One last thing that I want to discuss with you about taxes is ... *pay them.* Your practice will not grow if you are getting paid in cash under the table and not declaring this income for taxation. The square between 15° Scorpio (ruling taxes) and 15° Aquarius (ruling redistribution of resources) illustrates this metaphysical law. The midpoint of these two power degrees is 0° Capricorn, and by paying taxes on your income, willingly and conscientiously, your business will ascend the mountain of the sacred Goat.

Resale License and Sales Tax

Self-employed astrologers selling products other than their consultation services must charge, report and pay back state sales taxes. 45 of the 50 states in the U.S., plus the District of Columbia, have sales taxes. The states that do not are Alaska, Delaware, Montana, New Hampshire and Oregon.

If you are selling astrology books, calendars or other products that you buy at a wholesale price and then resell at a retail price, you must charge state sales tax for these items, then fill out the proper state and/or county reporting forms and include payment of taxes collected, as the law requires.

I presently live in Oregon, where we have no state sales tax, but I have had offices and practiced astrology in California, South Carolina and Washington State where I had to charge sales tax. You do not have to charge sales tax for class tuition, workshop tuition, consultations, or for out-of-state orders. But you must charge sales tax for in-state software sales, books and calendars.

In California, for example, you will need to get a *Seller's Permit* from the State Board of Equalization. This license needs to be displayed conspicuously at your place of business. When you are ordering products at wholesale prices, you will have to provide this number to the company you are buying from. Accounting methods using a spreadsheet for income should have a separate entry for the sales tax collected, so that you can fill out the quarterly state forms more efficiently.

Business Checking Account & Debit Card

The best way to handle your money as an astrologer is with a business checking account that comes with a VISA debit card, or *business check card*. Debit cards can be used just like credit cards, except that the money comes straight out of your checking account balance.

Recently, my bank discontinued the *PIN* procedure for my business check card, where a code could be entered to process a transaction, and now I must sign each time I use the debit card. The only exception to this is at the gas station, where the card can be swiped at the pump and a receipt is produced without a signature.

I have a *basic business checking* account with US Bank, and if my balance drops below $2000, I am charged a monthly maintenance fee of $8. If I write over 35 checks or make more than 15 electronic debit transactions, I get charged 15¢ for each one over the limit.

The monthly statement is well organized, with *deposits, debit card withdrawal* and *checks paid* all being clearly itemized. If a client writes a bad check, there is a $17 *NSF* (non-sufficient funds) charge levied to the account. I am happy to report that, with my Moon trine Venus, I have only had this occur twice in 13 years. I have been very fortunate to have had honest and responsible clients during my career.

If I bounce a check or make a debit card purchase that results in an overdrawn account, I am charged a *paid overdraft* fee of $27. I have had very good success with this bank, and I have been with them for over ten years now. It is also helpful to get to know your personal banker at your local branch, as they can be a true ally when you need to discuss a loan, or establish a merchant services account.

You can have your business checks printed with your company name in addition to your name, and many conversations at the cash register, and even a few clients have resulted from my check showing that I was an astrologer. My checks are printed like this:

> EARTHWALK SCHOOL OF ASTROLOGY
> ROBERT P. BLASCHKE, ASTROLOGER

Invoicing Clients, Past-Due Notices & Late Charges

For some self-employed astrologers, the least favorite task is collecting money from their clients. Most in-person clients will pay by check or cash, so this is not a problem. However, if you offer telephone consultation, taped readings by mail, or have a mail-order business for charts, reports and tapes, some payment issues will arise. Some astrologers will require a 50% deposit toward their consultation fee before they will even schedule an appointment.

If you decide to invoice for your professional services, rather than getting payment before the appointment, it is customary to be paid within 30 days. It is well within your rights to send a past-due notice if your invoice has not been paid by the end of the month following the month in which the appointment was scheduled. If, for example, you had a client on June 15, and had not received payment by July 31, it is appropriate for you to send a past due notice, and to add a late charge of 1.5%.

Paradoxically, it has been my experience that affluent clients are worse at paying on time than working-class clients. In their defense, their lives may be busier with travel, or their finances may be more complex, but that is no excuse. Astrologers should consider themselves professionals, and should be quite assertive in collecting consultation fees or mail-order invoice amounts owed to them.

I used to be known as *The Hammer* by my clients. With Aries on the cusp of my 8th house of other's money, which most Virgo risings possess, I was on the phone on the first day of the month following-up on any invoices that had gone unpaid for over 30 days. It took me a few years to get comfortable with this behavior, but the reality is that cash flow is extremely important for any self-employed individual, and it is just plain rude not to pay on time (Mars in Libra speaking here!).

Merchant Services Account

The best financial move I have ever made as an astrologer was to open a merchant services account with my bank. This account allows me to accept MasterCard or VISA as payment from clients and customers, money then electronically deposited into my business checking account the very same day. Think of it for a minute - no more invoices, no more late payments, and what great cash flow - a Scorpio dream!

However, there are bank charges and fees associated with these accounts. I will recap mine here for you:

1) Bankcard discount charges—I am charged between 2.75% and 4% per transaction plus 10¢ per item. A lowest discount of 2.75% applies when I swipe the credit card through my terminal; I am charged the middle rate of 3.5% when I get a telephone order with no physical credit card present, and enter the card number manually along with the customer's address and zip code; I am charged the highest rate of 4% when I get a telephone or e-mail order and cannot verify the customer's address.

2) I pay $24 per month to rent my *VISANET* terminal, and I pay $5 per year to rent my manual credit card imprinter, which I use on the road to accept credit cards for book sales and consultation fees. Then, I run the

transactions through electronically when I return to my office.

To give you an idea of the cost of this type of account, and what percentage of my overall business was paid by credit cards on a monthly basis, I will show you the following breakdown from my practice this year:

April 2001—$3095 gross income—$1836 paid by credit card—$64.45 in card fees
May 2001—$9354 gross income—$2104 paid by credit card—$79.43 in card fees
June 2001—$3706 gross income—$2072 paid by credit card—$72.43 in card fees
July 2001—$3740 gross income—$2009 paid by credit card—$70.18 in card fees

As you can see, other than in May, when I was extensively on the road lecturing, and was paid speaking and consultation fees mostly by cash or check, the credit card payments have been over 50% of my total gross during a typical month. I also had to pay my terminal rental fee of $24 each month.

The *bankcard discount*, or credit card fees, charged to this astrologer by the bank were only between 1.8% and 2% of my total gross income during a normal month. For me, it is well worth it to have a convenient and worry-free way to be paid. I have also been able to sell my books in over 20 different countries around the world, receiving e-mail orders which included the card number, expiration date and shipping address abroad.

To establish a merchant services account, I would recommend that you first apply for one at the same bank with which you have your business checking account. If you have formed a relationship with your personal banker, they can help push the application through the corporate headquarters. You will be asked certain questions on the application, such as what percentage of your business will result in *swiped card* transactions, and what percentage will be *mail/phone orders*.

Mail-order businesses are considered a higher risk for consumer fraud, and don't panic if you are turned down by your bank. There are independent companies out there that also offer merchant services accounts, and although their discount rates may be higher, after a few years of building a record of spotless transactions, you can get accepted by your bank.

One last thing that you should know about the merchant services accounts with the independent companies is that there is usually a two-day interchange delay before the money is deposited electronically into your business checking account. You will have to be extra careful not to bounce checks or debit purchases, thinking that you have funds in your account when in reality you do not until the next day.

Making Business Income Bank Deposits

Earlier in this chapter, in the section on creating spreadsheets, I outlined a method of preparing bank deposits. As a self-employed astrologer, you will have income from several different classifications; i.e. clients, tuition, books, reports, software commissions, etc. Your earnings will come in the form of cash, check, money order or credit card. I would advise you to make deposits twice a week, and to design a form on your computer that allows you to itemize these various income factors.

If you receive cash payment from clients regularly, you should deposit this money the very same day for two reasons: 1) *security* - don't walk around with hundred dollar bills; and 2) *temptation* - if you don't deposit that cash, you might spend it, and your bookkeeping will get sloppy.

I don't want to be your den mother, but the way you handle your money says a lot about how you respect yourself and your clients. Astrologers are professionals, and should view themselves in this way, and running a tight ship financially is how you build a successful practice. The temptation to avoid paying taxes is always there for self-employed individuals, especially when you are paid in cash, but you will feel like a hypocrite if you are dispensing spiritual guidance to your clients, yet not walking your talk with impeccability in your business finances.

My bank deposit form looks like this:

DATE	CLIENTS	SOFTWARE SALES	BOOKS	CHARTS/ REPORTS	WORK-SHOPS	CLASSES TUITION	TAPES/ SPEAKING	TOTAL DEPOSIT

While I am preparing each deposit, itemizing my income into the categories shown on the form above, in the lower half of the form I list subtotals for cash, check, money order or credit card. Then, if a teller at the bank should ever make an error in your deposit, you can go back to the bank with a precise breakdown of funds.

Electronic deposits are also available 24-7 through ATM machines, but I would only make deposits of checks in this way, and always take cash inside the bank. If you get a merchant services account, you will have to *batch* your deposits each day, a simple procedure of pushing a button on your terminal to get a daily report, then pushing the *transmit* button, which sends a deposit through your phone line.

Paying Yourself as a Sole-Proprietor

Reading this chapter, it may have occurred to you that we have been discussing an astrologer's business income. How do you pay your home rent or mortgage? How do you buy your groceries and clothes? How do you make your car payment? The answer is that, as a sole proprietor, you will need to pay yourself a salary from your net income. Most astrologers will have a second, personal checking account, so that they can separate between business and non-business purchases.

This payment to yourself can be made bimonthly or monthly. You simply write a check from your business account to yourself, and then deposit it into your personal account as if it were a paycheck. Some astrologers will even have a third account in which they set aside money for paying their estimated quarterly taxes. I recommend pulling 6% of your gross each month to deposit into your tax account.

Cash Flow, Business Loans & Carrying Debt

The self-employed astrologer will need to understand the concept of cash flow, or wind up in the asylum on thorazine with a nervous breakdown. When you leave a secure paycheck behind, and enter the unknown land of uncertain income, you have essentially undertaken a financial firewalk of epic spiritual proportions.

Most self-employed individuals describe how their energy directly affects the amount of money they are making. If you are moody like me, with six planets plus a south node in water signs, your income is likely to fluctuate wildly from week to week or from month to month. If you are an earthy soul, with four planets in Taurus or Capricorn, you may be able to achieve a stable and predictable income as a professional astrologer.

Cash flow in your private practice is best understood by viewing income from a monthly, quarterly, or even yearly perspective, rather than daily or weekly. The reality is that an astrologer can make $375 on Tuesday, and not a dime on Friday. Clients can be scheduled in appointment bunches, and then you may be writing for several days without a drop of income. Your mind will need to get adjusted to this concept, so that you will not exhaust yourself by worrying about money.

I have been at this for 13 years, and I still have not figured out cash flow. I have had weeks where I made $2300, and then the next week I made $165. It used to drive me nuts - think Scorpio control issues here - and I so wanted to be able to know what to expect moneywise each month. I have had to learn that not all the work I do today pays me today.

For example, I might spend two days writing an article. Then, it is not published in a magazine or journal for another six months. Three months after it appears in the publication, I might get calls from individuals wanting to schedule a telephone consultation. They then become regular clients and I hear from them once or twice a year for many years afterwards. This scenario depicts how today's labor of writing, while not producing immediate earnings, plants seeds for future income.

Through the years, it has dawned on me that astrology is a calling, not a job. And, as such, it requires a radically different attitude toward money in order to become financially successful. I have had to learn how to put my clients first, my students first, or my contribution to the profession as an author first, in order for the income to happen naturally. Trust and faith seem to be the two horses pulling the chariot of astrological income.

If you step back and look at your income quarterly, you will see how hundreds, and even thousands of dollars can just sit in your business checking account until it is needed for the payment of rent, your phone bill, the next trip to Office Depot, or whatever. The last thing that you want to do is to divide your monthly gross income by the number of hours that you spent in your office, thus creating a false perception of an hourly wage.

Astrologers are like lawyers or real estate agents, who may go weeks without pay until they land a commission or a retainer for their work. But, they don't starve, and they learn to salt some bucks away when they are flush, just like a squirrel puts some nuts away for the long and cold winter.

It is said that it takes money to make money (must have been a Taurus, don't you think?). A self-employed astrologer trying to expand a practice may have to take out a business loan to get to the next level. When I started my publishing company in 1998, my secondary progressed Sun was squaring my natal Mars. My attitude was: *whatever it takes.*

I have written two books before this one, and each has gone to a second printing. I have been able to pay the printer out of my cash flow on three of the four printings and have only had to borrow money once. I have been carrying this debt of $6000 since June 1999, and have made one payment of $1500, with $4500 yet to go.

I have learned that business debt is different than personal debt, because it is for a larger cause than personal need or gratification. I have made a commitment to my publishing company, one where I will write seven astrology volumes between my Saturn opposition, at age 44-45, and my second Saturn return at age 59. The debt will be paid back, and will have served to build a foundation.

Self-employed astrologers who leave the corporate world in their 30's to begin a practice sometimes have savings or a profit-sharing payout from an employer to hold them over until they can build the astrology income. In due time, waking up broke one day with no resources to cover the unpredictable income swings other than guts and perseverance, they now find themselves going through the baptism of Saturn. *How bad do you want it? Can I endure?* If I can do it, you can do it.

Chapter Four

Marketing & Advertising

Setting up your professional practice is like baking a cake from scratch. You will need a variety of ingredients, in proper proportion and quantity, to arrive at a tasty finished product. When you go into business as an astrologer, you are selling yourself and your professional services. How do you now make the community aware of the availability of your work?

The marketing of your astrology practice will need to draw on the qualities of your natal Jupiter and Saturn in order to be successful. Advertising your services will ideally reflect the virtues of your natal Mercury and your third house ruler. Marketing differs from advertising in that its goal is to create a professional image, a sort of Midheaven packaging, if you will.

One is known personally as an individual through his Ascendant, but when one begins a private practice, the Midheaven kicks in as your professional persona. The tenth house rules one's business, as well as your reputation and stature, and, therefore, the best marketing that you can do for your practice is through the energies of your culminating sign, your Jupiter sign, and your Saturn sign.

For example, I have Virgo rising, and am appreciated by my clients for using impeccable technique as an astrologer, with an attitude of spiritual service. But, I also have a Gemini Midheaven, and I am known professionally for the versatility of my astrology practice, which includes being an author and lecturer, a school, a publishing company, a mail-order business, a software dealer, and a catalogue of lecture and class tapes in addition to my consultation work.

Advertising, on the other hand, is more Mercurial. You will have to go into your local and regional environments and search out connections and opportunities for yourself and your work as an astrologer. With my Mercury in Scorpio, I have advertised my practice to psychotherapists and their clients, to metaphysicians of all sorts and stripes, and to small businesses for help in their financial decisions.

I will share my experiences with marketing and advertising, and give a summary of the different methods and ideas I have used to sell my work in the community. Not all have produced the results that I wanted, and I will be honest with you about this. Although your experience may differ, I hope mine will help you avoid some unnecessary expense on the road to building your successful astrology practice.

I will discuss yellow page ads, alternative practitioner directories, display and classified ads, bulk-mailings, the Internet, media appearances, and the *shoe leather approach* to marketing (where you pound the pavement and put your business cards, brochures and flyers wherever you can find empty space on bulletin boards around town).

Family, Friends & Co-workers

The obvious place to start advertising your new practice is with everyone that you already know. This includes your family and relatives, all of your friends, and your co-workers and colleagues. This group of people will surprise you with how much business they can bring your way. Astrology is a *personal service*, and a new client is more likely to come to you if they know someone who knows you.

However, there is a line of good taste here that should not be crossed. You do not want to start out like you are one of those annoying New Agers selling the latest multi-level cabal that will revolutionize your life for just $499. Discreetly, you can inform your family, friends and co-workers that you are now accepting clients, and ask them to make others aware of this.

If you have been doing astrology for free with relatives, while you were employed and did not need to earn money from it, you will now have to set some necessary professional boundaries and begin to charge for your services. Don't be bashful here; you will, in fact, be more respected as a professional for doing this, and there is a common perception that what is free is of less value than what is paid for.

When I began my full-time astrology practice in 1989, after practicing part-time since 1979, I made many new clients through the 12-Step recovery groups that I was attending, such as Co-Dependents Anonymous and Adult Children of Alcoholics. Crews of us used to go out for dinner or coffee after the meetings, and I was the guy with the three-ring binder full of everyone's birthchart, and was just about mobbed with interested parties wanting to schedule an appointment. They were my friends and brought me much business.

Referrals

The irony in practicing astrology is that the best advertising is always free. You can get one extroverted air or fire sign individual that you have a splendid consultation with and they will refer you to dozens of their friends, relatives and co-workers. You can conversely spend hundreds of dollars on advertising that does not bring one single new client. I had to adjust to this reality. With my Sun inconjunct Jupiter, I had a belief that advertising *always* would produce business.

When you walk into a restaurant, you will sometimes see a little sign that says: *If you like the service, tell others; if you don't, tell us.* This is a good business model for professional astrologers to build a practice with. At the end of a consultation, you will have a few minutes of social pleasantries while a client is writing you the check, and you are putting the charts and tape into an envelope.

This is a time for you to tell your client that you hope they got everything that was expected from the appointment, and that you would appreciate any referrals. If the client has anything that made them unhappy during the consultation, this creates a safe post-discussion environment for them to inform you of any disappointments. I feel that this sort of *client relations* management will serve you well.

I get referrals from people all over the country who have never even met me, but have either read my books or have had a telephone consultation with me. One client that had an in-person appointment with me in 1989, then went to school for many years and eventually became a psychiatric nurse. After she started working at a Bay Area hospital almost *ten years later* she referred one co-worker to me for a telephone consultation who, in turn, referred over a dozen others!

Establishing an Advertising Budget

How much money should an astrologer spend on advertising? As I mentioned in Chapter Three, one is taught in business school that a marketing budget should not exceed 6-7% of your total gross revenues. To bring this abstract concept down to earth for an astrologer, let's look at the economics of this equation.

If you charge $100 for a consultation, then 6-7% of that is $6-$7. Thus, for the ideal return on your advertising dollar, each $100 of ad money spent should bring in $1400 to $1700 worth of client consultations. This would be equivalent to scheduling 14 to 17 appointments at $100 each.

The reality is that initial advertising will not usually bring about these results. In marketing theory, it is *repetition, brand name awareness* and *multiple visibility* that produce results. And time is an essential ingredient for these factors to mature. The astrologer will have to stick with his chosen advertising to accomplish repetition, keep his name out there to create brand name awareness, and have at least three ads running at a time to produce multiple visibility.

If you diversify your practice to include teaching classes and workshops, selling charts, reports and software, and having books and tapes available for purchase, then each new customer can bring in greater income for you because they have more to buy from you. Then, your *advertising dollar to income ratio* works.

Yellow Page Ads

For many years, I maintained a box ad in the yellow pages of the phone directory. Under the heading of *Astrologers* each year, there were six or seven of us that had ads. Some astrologers, or those selling astrology-related products such as Zodiac jewelry, would just have a single line ad which was a complimentary listing for having business phone service.

Some of the line ads would be in bold print, or have a second line below the name and phone number, and the astrologer would have to spend about $15 a month for these enhancements. I always chose, with Jupiter on my MC, to have a 3/4 inch or 1 inch box ad that stood me out from the pack. In this ad, I could have five lines of text in addition to my address and phone number. I paid $68.10 a month for the ad.

Over the years, I got plenty of calls from my yellow page ad that resulted in new clients and students. However, I also got weirdo calls leaving stoned and drunken messages on my voice-mail at 3:30 AM. In addition, I would get John or Jane Q. Public calling me for information on meteor showers, where they could buy Zodiac key chains, or the good old *hey dude, when's that full moon happenin'?* calls.

To be honest with you, I never received the return on my investment directly from this ad that justified spending $817 per year. Some months I would get 20-25 callers identifying themselves as having seen the yellow page ad, and other months less than 5. That said, I will never know how much my ad in the yellow pages contributed to the *multiple visibility* theory of marketing, with clients calling me because they had seen my name in one or two other publications.

My advice for an astrologer just starting out would be to have a yellow page ad, which would in turn require business phone service. Astrologers are not quite the same as plumbers. If a person's sewer is backing up and coming through the bathtub drain, one instinctively reaches for the phone book to find the number for Roto-Rooter. But, our services *are* needed in the community, and many people use the yellow pages to shop and see what *is* available out there.

Because of my yellow page ad, I have been on television several times. Local TV news stations have contacted me because a reporter saw my ad under *Astrologers* and called to ask for an interview, to be shown later on the evening newscast. I would be asked about Friday the 13th lore, Full Moons, Eclipses and other astronomical phenomena on which they thought I could elucidate and wax poetically. From a half-hour taping, after the guy in the editing room got done with me, I was on TV for about 90 seconds.

Alternative Practitioner Directories

Most progressive large urban areas and hip small college towns have alternative directories of healing arts practitioners. Astrologers can place listings in these publications to advertise their practice, and many of these bimonthly or quarterly magazines also have a matching website version of the print issuance. They are usually distributed at places like bookstores or health food stores, which have racks or shelves for free newspapers and magazines. Their claims of circulation numbers are generally exaggerated, as many unread copies find the recycling bins.

In Portland, we had publications such as *Reflections* and *Community ConneXion* in which I placed listings. The directory ads had information about my practice, school and the other astrological services that I offered such as charts, reports and software. I had several clients and students find me through these ads, and the cost was quite reasonable; about $49 for a bimonthly placement.

Sometimes, directories have editorial content, and an astrologer can write columns or articles for them. If they cannot pay you for the writing, you can negotiate a trade for advertising. The holistic healing community is commonly tightly knit, and referral networks can easily emerge for you by getting known within it. Many of the clients that you get from advertising in these publications will be healers such as rolfers, chiropractors, acupuncturists, massage therapists and the like.

I have done a fair amount of medical diagnosis as an astrologer. Once this fact became known amongst the various healing arts practitioners listed in these directories, a lot of business was sent to me.

One of the better success stories I have regarding these directories came as a result of my listing on the website version of a publication. I was contacted by a metaphysical church in Salem, Oregon, and asked to teach astrology classes to the congregation members. In the Fall of 1999, I taught my eight-week beginning astrology class at this church; and in the Spring of 2000, I was brought back again to teach my eight-week intermediate class.

The nine students, along with the Reverend, were some of the most delightful people I have ever taught, and all very motivated to learn astrology. In addition to selling my books and software there, I scheduled a fair number of consultations with them, as well.

Display & Classified Ads

You probably don't want to hear how much money I have spent on magazine display ads over the years. Possibly, it would have been enough for a down payment on a medium-sized house. Whether or not I would be where I am today as an astrologer, without having spent this money on advertising, is an unanswered question in my mind.

In 1991, I began to more aggressively market computerized astrology reports. I had previously been selling natal interpretations, using the new Chart Interpreter program from Time Cycles' Gamma Edition for the Macintosh, but then had acquired software to produce relationship reports and transit forecasts.

At first, I was just selling these to my clients locally and regionally; then I started to place low-cost display ads with various publications in Portland to market the reports more widely. In 1992, I earned $2397 selling reports and spent $762 on total advertising costs. During 1993, I earned $5356 selling reports and had spent

$2247 on advertising.

The other investments I made to gear up for this extra business were for a laser printer, a merchant services account to be able to accept credit card purchases, and a toll-free order number. Once this infrastructure was in place, I decided to go national with the mail-order business. Oh, the woes of Jupiter on the Midheaven!

In 1994, I started display ads in the *Utne Reader* magazine which cost $720 every two months. The ad had my Earthwalk Astrology logo, my 800 number, my post office box mailing address, and a concise description of the three reports that I was selling. I charged $25 per report, and shipping charges were added. The phone started ringing with credit card orders, and every day was like Christmas at the post office, with checks showing up in the mail.

My trusty 1993 HP LaserJet 4ML printer (which I still have!) was cranking out ream after ream of pages, 4 per minute, and I organized the production down to a science. I had blue report covers with my logo on them, a heavy duty stapler, white plastic spines to cover the edges, and a very professional-looking product to ship to my customers. I earned $10,146 selling reports in 1994 with advertising costs of $4110. In 1995, I sold $10,743 worth of reports with total ad costs of $5241.

I should state here that additional advertising, (such as ads in *The Mountain Astrologer* and other magazines), along with my newsletters, were part of these marketing costs. It was hard for me to track additional business coming in as a result of this, such as consultations that were subsequently scheduled by report customers. Report order forms were included with my newsletter mailings to ± 2000 clients.

After my *Utne Reader* ad contract expired, I placed the same ad in *New Age Journal* for $340 bimonthly. During 1996, I earned $9191 selling reports, with advertising costs of $3950. It was during this fourth year of selling reports, in addition to a very demanding consulting practice *and* teaching classes two to three nights a week, plus Saturday workshops, that I was approaching burnout. I had to come up for air to analyze the realistic profitability of my entire astrology business.

After closely examining my financial spreadsheets, I saw that as my gross income increased, my expenses had also gone way up, leaving me with a net income relatively unchanged. I realized that I could take the energy I was spending to sustain my mail-order business of selling reports nationally and use it creatively to write my books.

As a result of intentionally de-emphasizing report sales, in 1997 I sold $6717 worth of reports, $4824 in 1998, $4888 in 1999, $3318 in 2000, and only $1100 this year. I learned that display ads in national magazines do actually work quite well if you are trying to develop a mail-order business, but in the long run, you may find that you are just trading dollars. For every new dollar of increased gross income that comes in, there may be close to the same amount being spent, which leaves your net income flat.

My annual advertising costs have been steadily dropping since I made a decision to start writing books, build my publishing company and let go of the report sales. After a peak of spending over $5000 on advertising during 1995, my yearly totals have been $3950 in 1996, $4696 in 1997, $1113 in 1998, $2956 in 1999, $2143 in 2000, and about $1540 for 2001. Jupiter is known to rule over-extension and excesses, and with it conjunct my MC, I have had to learn to *just say no.*

To test my astrology practice against the recommended business school formula of 6-7% of total revenues being spent on advertising, let's do the math together here. In the ten years, 1992-2001, I have grossed $321,718 as an astrologer. My total advertising costs for those same ten years is $28,758. This equals 8.94% of my gross, which puts me in the Jupiter column of having spent a little too much.

A more modest approach to building your astrology business would be to place classified ads in lieu of display ads. Although not as flashy, these cost much less, and can still fulfill your three requirements of marketing theory, namely *repetition, brand name awareness* and *multiple visibility.* For example, the display ad for my publishing company in *The Mountain Astrologer* costs me $220 for a 1/4 page layout. *TMA* has inexpensive classified ads available for $30-$60 per insertion, giving you 30 to 75 words of text.

I placed a classified ad in *Portland Parent* to market my natal interpretation reports for children. It produced some consistent business for me after it ran in repeated bimonthly issues, and it only cost $18.90.

Circulating Brochures & Business Cards

The self-employed astrologer on a shoestring budget, without enough income yet to cover the costs of advertising, can still market his practice the old-fashioned way by using the *shoe leather approach.* With this method you pound the pavement and put your brochures and business cards in lobbies, waiting rooms, reception areas and on public information tables at bookstores and natural food stores, etc.

In Chapter Two, I wrote about how to make brochures and business cards with inexpensive supplies purchased from Office Depot. With a computer and printer, you can produce professional-looking marketing materials that can be circulated around town. For starters, I recommend using the yellow pages to make a list of different locations you want to target with this effort.

Write down names and phone numbers of libraries, bookstores, healing centers, natural food stores, psychic institutes, metaphysical centers, therapy offices and any other environments that you think would have an interest in astrology. Then, before you go there, call first to introduce yourself as a professional astrologer, and ask if you can drop by and leave some advertising materials. Making personal contact initially by phone is much better than just stopping by unannounced.

Also, before you take your printed materials to these locations, go to Office Depot and buy some clear plastic business card holders and vertical brochure stands. This will make a good impression. Many of these places, such as bookstores and waiting rooms at healing centers, have quite a few advertising materials already strewn about, and placing your brochures in one of these stands will set apart your literature from the rest. The same is true for the business card holders.

Don't forget that this is not a one-stop marketing effort. You should go back every two weeks to check on and replenish your materials, and keep a dated checklist of each place where you have dropped off your items. I found that other practitioners can be pretty devious in the Darwinian struggle for name exposure. I repeatedly saw that my brochures had been taken out of their plastic stand and replaced with some other healer's material. Being a Scorpio, you can be sure that they were immediately called and reprimanded for this transgression.

I have an amazing and literal brochure-circulation story to tell you! In 1991, I had put some of my literature in a little book and gift store called Moonshadows, now long out of business. They were in an eclectic neighborhood in Portland called Multnomah Village, which had shops, cafes and small local businesses.

I lovingly had put my brochures on a table near the front door. A woman moved to Portland from Texas shortly thereafter. One windy day in the Fall, as she was walking down Capitol Highway, the main street that this store was on, a gust of wind blew one of my brochures out the door and it swirled down and into her hands. I swear to God that I am not making this up.

She had been an astrology student in Houston, and after receiving this windy manna from heaven, she took it as a sign that I was the man to see. I will never forget the day she showed up at one of my workshops, sitting on the floor in front of me with rapt attention. It was only later that I learned of how she had found me, and the significance she felt.

Flyers & Bulletin Boards

At many of these same locations, you will find that there are also corkboards and bulletin boards available for public notices, both inside the building and just outside the main entry. Here you can put up flyers that you have designed on your computer announcing your classes, consultations or chart and report services. As with your brochures and business cards, it will be better to call first and speak to the person who manages these bulletin boards before you show up.

Some of the bookstores will require you to datestamp your flyers, as this is how they keep these bulletin boards organized and current. Sometimes, they even give you a bus ticket punch to put little round holes in the corners of your flyers, and then you would hang them on cupboard hooks screwed into the horizontal slats.

I have advertised my classes and workshops with flyers at libraries, bookstores, therapy office waiting rooms, healing center reception areas and the like, and I got to know the individuals who looked after the free literature areas with repeated visits there. A brief chat with them about who you are and your work as an astrologer can lead to referrals and recommendations to you by them.

Try to get into the habit of always carrying business cards, brochures and flyers with you in your car, or laptop carrying case if you are hoofing it. Even in cafes, food markets and coffee houses, there will be bulletin boards, sometimes back by the payphones near the bathrooms, and you will be surprised at how these obscure locations can prove the marketing theory of *multiple visibility*. I had clients who, when they called to schedule a first appointment, said they had heard about me from two different people, and then saw my card next to the ladies room at a restaurant, and took that as a sign from Spirit to contact me!

Newsletters & Client Birthday Mailings

In Chapter Two, I wrote about data base software and how it has been at the heart of my astrology business for the last ten years. The self-employed astrologer can enter all pertinent client information into a data base. Such a program is only as good as the care with which it is maintained, and the *skillful field creation* that goes into it at the beginning.

I also wrote about bulk-mail permits and how to send out mailings using standard rates, which are cheaper than first class postage. In 1992, I began publishing a quarterly Earthwalk Astrology newsletter. In it, I had my schedule of classes and workshops, information about my consultation services, and a letter to my clients and students. I used the same color paper (blue) for ten years in a row, and the 8.5" x 11" newsletter also had my report and tape order forms included.

I would fold it in half as a three or four-page piece of mail, staple it and put a mailing label on the outside that included my return address and permit account number. I would also occasionally include UAC or ISAR conference brochures in these bulk-mailings, as the postage was the same all the way up to 3.3 ounces.

As a faculty member at ISAR conferences, I would be part of a profit-sharing program which, if the conference made money, paid the speakers *shares* for lecturing and for helping to promote the conference by including brochures in their mailings. I recall one happy day at the post office when I was almost broke and a check for $461 came from the ISAR treasurer, three months after the conference.

I would presort my data base numerically by zip code and then print sheets of thirty self-adhesive mailing labels. These were accomplished by using the *print merge* feature in the software. With your data base program open, you could then create a template page for 30 mailing labels by selecting the name, address, city, state and zip code fields, and placing them in 3 lines. Then, when you chose *print merge,* the program would make labels for every person in your data base.

According to postal requirements, I would arrange the bulk-mailing into rubber-banded bundles of newsletters all going to the same 3 or 5 digit zip codes, or to the same area distribution centers. These mail pieces would then be organized and placed into cardboard or plastic trays, which were then put inside a cardboard sleeve and held snug with plastic tie strapping.

With my Mercury accidentally dignified in my third house, ruling post offices and postal workers, I used to actually quite enjoy this project every three months. I had the reputation at the Lake Oswego post office as the most efficient (think Virgo rising) bulk-mailer in town, and I loved those guys and gals at my local post office. Some were Vietnam vets, some were musicians with a day job, and my experience through the years with the US Postal Service has been nothing but a delight.

These newsletter mailings were a three-day project for me, where I would just disappear for awhile until it was done, with no clients scheduled and letting the phone calls ring into voice-mail. After I wrote and formatted my newsletter and printed the originals, I would then go to Office Depot, which had the lowest copy prices in town at 2¢ each for 1000 or more, and have the whole job high-speed copied. These guys were great, with the copy job being done usually that same day, and I would buy reams of colored Xerox copy paper at the store for each page.

The five-foot folding table that I described in Chapter Two under *Office Furniture* was the center of activity for this project. Spread out around me would be stacks of the copied pages, my stapler, rubber bands, the mailing label sheets and a postal service publication showing the zip code sorting requirements.

Sometimes, if I was lucky, a girlfriend would come to my office with a picnic basket and some cold beer, feeding me and getting me just hazed enough to take the monotony out of it. I usually wound up doing 98% of the actual work myself, but I do have fond memories of bread and cheese and beer and laughter. I always wondered if my newsletter recipients could feel the love that went into it.

As an advertising tool and marketing vehicle, my quarterly newsletters would always bring a spike in business, with tape or report order forms being filled out and returned with a check in the mail. My clients would keep up with the latest heartache or happiness in my personal odyssey, and I would get several calls from them for appointment scheduling. My mailing list got as high as 2300 addresses.

If you want to maintain a clean mailing list for your newsletters, you must bite the bullet and pay extra for notification from the postal service, which forwards the mail piece to a client that has moved, and then sends you a standard form showing the new address. I must warn you, however, that this gets expensive.

To do so, print *Address Service Requested* underneath your return address. You must get a *postage due account* with the post office. When each mail piece is forwarded to clients that moved, you receive a form with the new address, and for a year after the move a 60¢ *address correction fee* will be charged to your account.

From 13 to 18 months after your client moves, the letter will not be forwarded, but returned with the new address attached, and you will be charged a *weighted fee.* 18 months or more after the move, the letter is returned marked *undeliverable,* and you will likewise be charged the weighted return fee (as much as 80-90¢).

A slightly less expensive way to keep your mailing list lean, mean and clean is to print *Change Service Requested* under your return address, and the postal service will not forward it, but throw away the letter and only send you the notice of a new address. They will charge you the address correction fee of 60¢.

As you can see, this gets expensive. To give an idea of my newsletter production and mailing costs, this is an itemized breakdown for a 3-pager mailing of 1500:

a) 9 reams of colored copy paper @ 5.00 per ream = $45
b) 3000 single-sided copies @ 2¢ per = $60
c) 1500 double-sided copies @ 3.5¢ per = $52.50
d) ± 750 letters @ DSCF basic standard postage rate of 22.9¢ per = $171.75
e) ± 750 letters @ DSCF 3/5 digit zip standard postage rate of 20.9¢ per = $156.75
f) total production and mailing costs = $486
   [DSCF = District Sectional Carrier Facility; a discount is given for bringing bulk-mailings here]

In addition, you also have to pay $125 per year for a standard mail permit (10 years ago this was $75 a year, and has risen to $85, $100 and now $125); and a one-time charge of $125 for a permit imprint, so that you do not have to affix stamps to the letters. If you send out four newsletters a year, then this adds an extra $31.25 ($125 ÷ 4) to your per-mailing costs, and doesn't include the address correction fees.

Using the ideal *advertising to income ratio* of 6-7% of the gross, this means that, for a $517 total newsletter cost, I should get $7954 in business from it ($517 ÷ .065). At four of these a year, that would be $31,816 gross income ($7954 x 4) for $2068 worth of newsletter mailings ($517 x 4). To be honest with you, I don't think I ever had anywhere near this kind of return on my newsletter advertising investment, but who can say what the value was of my consistent mailings and the resultant loyalty of my client base?

I will give you a tip for pruning your mailing list, which will help to keep your postal service address correction fees under control. Over the years, I have had a field in my data base for *Address Change,* and I would put a notation in it for the date of any client having moved (i.e. 12/01 or 7/99, etc.). I found that my report customers were likely to move much more frequently than my consultation clients, resulting in fees charged to me by the post office for forwarding the newsletter.

I also noticed that these report customers were usually one-time purchasers, with no subsequent orders coming in no matter how long I kept sending newsletters. At last, I got wise to this, and started to cut them out of my data base 6 months after their report purchase if they did not buy anything else or schedule a consultation.

On the other hand, my consultation clients have had a history of lasting and stable addresses, along with consistent repeat business through the years. This brings up an economic theory that I have as an astrologer: *you are better off with 400 regular clients for whom you take meticulous care of their needs, than to have a data base of 2000 people that purchase services or products from you sporadically or once only.*

One other promotional tool I have used is client birthday mailings. I offer a modest discount (10%) as an incentive for scheduling a consultation. Most regular clients who have been with me for many years usually call around their birthdays to book appointments. Presort the *Birthday* field in your data base and you can pull out the Novembers or Decembers and send out a targeted mailing to these clients.

E-Mail Mass Mailings

With the rapid rise of e-mail as the favored correspondence for many clients, a modern self-employed astrologer now finds himself presented with new choices of how to spend his advertising dollars. As you have seen in the preceding section on print newsletters, they are costly and time-consuming; and keeping your mailing list current requires a lot of effort.

Many astrologers nowadays, myself included, are switching over to electronic newsletters to save on postage, paper and printing costs. The question remains: *Will these e-mailed newsletters be read?* A letter in the mail is still more likely to be examined than an e-mail.

With the proliferation of attachment file technology, it is quite simple to format your newsletter as you always did, attach it to an e-mail, and send it to everyone in your Internet address book.

Realistically, there are problems that can occur with opening attached files. Many clients may have older computers without the applications necessary to do this; also cross-platform headaches between PC's and Apple may hinder your efforts. A solution to this problem is to copy and paste the newsletter directly into an e-mail.

An additional worry is the *hatred of spam* that abounds these days. Many people perceive unrequested e-mail correspondence as if it were junk-mail, and take a perverse delight in deleting it and then sending it to the electronic trash can.

So, what should the astrologer do? I will share with you my experience of sending out mass e-mails to promote my books, announce classes, publication dates or speaking schedules, or to send articles that I have written to everyone in my electronic address book.

Presently, I have 1450 e-mail addresses of clients, students, book customers and astrological friends and colleagues. Where did all these addresses come from? For the last five years I have meticulously collected them from different sources. Whenever I get an e-mail inquiry about my professional services or about my books, or regular correspondence from another astrologer, I copy and paste the address into my mailing list alphabetically.

I have also received mass e-mailings from various astrologers selling software or other products and services. These senders may have websites that surreptitiously collect the e-mail addresses of anyone coming to their site. Some of these e-mails were not sent to me using the *Bcc selection* (blind carbon copy), and all of the addressees were visible, so I copied and pasted them into my growing collection.

The first time that I sent a mass e-mail was in June 1999, to announce the second printing of *Volume I*, and to thank those who had purchased a copy from the first printing. It was, in my opinion, a benign e-mail containing factual information along with book review excerpts, and perhaps a slight bit of pride in my work.

Some stressed-out astrologer in Michigan, perhaps having just escaped from a neurorehab center the day before, took umbrage with my e-mail, and another that she had just received. Presuming that her address had been taken from an ISAR directory (it wasn't), she proceeded to pepper the ISAR webmistress and journal editor with vociferous complaints about spam, comparing the likes of me with eliminative body parts, dinnertime telemarketers and panhandlers. Ouch!

Needless to say, the ISAR board went into a tizzy over what to do about e-mail marketing efforts such as these, and brought the issue out into the public arena for a pros and cons discussion. I was duly reprimanded, and I rebutted with my point of view that if I had been selling Zodiac T-shirts or coffee mugs, I could justify this ballistic reaction, but this was a book about a major astrological technique, and for God's sake, woman, just use your delete button in your e-mail software!

Since then, I have sent out mass e-mailings with the following content:

a) March 2000: requesting research volunteers for Volume II
b) December 2000: announcing the publication of Volume II
c) March 2001: announcing an East Coast speaking schedule
d) August 2001: announcing an ONLINE College of Astrology class
e) September 2001: a trilogy of articles on the 9/11 terrorist attack
f) October 2001: an epilogue on the terrorist attack and two subsequent articles
g) December 2001: announcing online classes and an East Coast speaking schedule

I now write a notice at the bottom of each mass e-mailing which reads:

****

IF YOU WISH TO BE REMOVED FROM THIS ELECTRONIC
NEWSLETTER E-MAILING ADDRESS LIST, CLICK REPLY
AND TYPE "REMOVE" IN THE SUBJECT FIELD

****

The irony is that to send out mass e-mailings, there is just as much follow-up work needed to maintain a clean e-mail address list as there is in maintaining a postal mailing list. Many e-mails will get bounced back to you as being undeliverable with a bad address. These must be deleted from your list, along with those addresses of individuals who have asked you to remove them from your mailings.

I have had positive experiences with these mass e-mailings. My articles have been copied, pasted and forwarded to other's mailing lists around the world. Talk about exponential cyber distribution!

Consequently, I have received scores of e-mails from recipients of these *forwards,* requesting to be added to my mailing list, or for my permission to reprint the copyrighted articles on a website. One astrologer even sent me a check for $200 to publish my articles on her site. In addition, I scheduled many phone consultations as a result of sending out my terrorist attack articles in September 2001.

I have decided to no longer send print newsletters, but to contact my clients via e-mail instead. The only exception will be to send out a targeted mailing for this and future volumes to those who have bought my books directly from me in the past. I will send one of these mailings each year to keep my data base current, and I will use first class postage in lieu of renewing my *standard mail* permit for $125 a year.

Building a Website

I am the wrong guy to write this section of the chapter, as I have passionately and conscientiously avoided a website to sell myself. Most days, I stand at the edge of the Internet, peering into a world that I consider to be utter madness and the prime culprit of social and cultural disintegration, using it only for e-mail, teaching classes at *ONLINE College of Astrology,* or to check my book sales at *Amazon.com.*

It is my conjecture that technology conspirators have the world hoodwinked into thinking that cyber-community may actually contribute any lasting value to the human condition. That said, like any hypocritical environmentalist still driving a car while he waxes political about the Arctic tundra, I must be careful here with my opinion, as I use this technology daily, albeit sparingly, for my own purposes.

What I am trying to obliquely say here, is that I would rather give a public lecture at an astrology salon in my own home, attracting new clientele who have heard me speak in the warmth of a living room, than to build a website and get e-mail from some faceless soul in South America or Iceland. How can I adequately provide my services to them?

Many astrologers have swarmed like bees to the Internet, building websites, linking themselves to other sites, and creating a proliferation of free astrological information that has saturated cyberspace. In my view, the Internet has created an intellectual decline in astrology of historical proportions.

Knowledge is ideally disseminated through a hierarchy, and the basic weakness of the Internet is the horizontal circulation of astrological lore with no editorial discernment or scrutiny to separate the wheat from the chaff. Now that this insane Genie has been let out of the bottle, I have no idea how astrology as a profession can ever return to a systematic dissemination of erudition and scholarship.

Therefore, because of my absence of experience with web design or construction, I will refer my readers who want to investigate building a website to market and advertise their astrology practice to the chapter entitled Using the Internet to Expand Your Practice from *How to Start, Maintain and Expand an Astrological Practice;* © 2001 by Rick Levine; The Organization for Professional Astrology; ISBN 0-9700696-2-6; www.professional-astrology.org; 941.261.2840.

Media Appearances

Another marketing vehicle for the self-employed astrologer is radio or television appearances. I have been on TV several times, both cable and network affiliate stations, and I have also been interviewed on the radio many times. My experience is that, while this certainly looks good on a resumé, practically speaking it did not result in much new business, if any at all.

As I wrote earlier in this chapter, under the section on yellow page ads, I have been called several times by local news stations. The reporters would ask to come to my office to tape interviews with me about an upcoming solar eclipse, Full Moon, or one time, about the origins of Friday the 13th! It occurred to me that my ad under the *Astrologers* heading in the yellow pages must have implied to the reporter that I have expertise in *general spooky subjects.*

Attempting to represent my profession with a smidgen of respectability, I would go to the men's room before they arrived and tuck in my shirt and comb my hair a bit. Eloquently I would discourse about this or that, tying it all together with a unified spiritual theme, hoping that perhaps three people in their living rooms that night would know what I might be talking about.

I would get a few calls the next day from clients who saw me while chewing their tofu cutlets at dinnertime, as my familiar face came onto their screen. Laughing at me, they told me how the guys in the editing room had werewolf visuals and some pathetic music from a B-grade horror movie as the lead-in, and then there I was, talking about Friday the 13th with some kind of cobweb frame surrounding me like I was Gomez from the Addams Family. Why didn't I go into law or medicine?

My colleague, Diana Stone, and I made some joint appearances on TV in Portland many years ago. I had been initially contacted by a gentleman who was developing a cable television show about alternative healing, and he was filming it in the studios of a local community college. I asked if I could bring a colleague to join me, as a way of spreading the exposure, if you will, and he agreed. She and I had a lot of fun doing this show, and I was invited back several times.

Diana and I were also invited to appear on the *AM Northwest* show, produced by a network affiliate station in Portland. I also appeared on that show many other times with one or two fellow astrologers. Once, around Valentine's Day, they invited three of us to tell women in the viewing audience how to attract love from men, going through each of the twelve Sun signs. It was all very lighthearted and glib, and at least I hadn't been cast like Uncle Fester or Lurch.

My reasoning of why my TV appearances brought no business is the audience that the shows were targeting. People watching daytime TV, or an obscure cable channel with a viewing audience the size of a crowded tavern, were not likely to become an astrology client. Additionally, the portrayal an astrologer receives on television is sometimes more likely to result in mockery than professional respect.

I will leave you with a funny anecdote from Diana's silver tongue. Once, when she was on the *AM Northwest* show, the male co-host, also the weatherman on the nightly news, asked her snidely just before the commercial break how often her predictions were accurate. As the camera was on his face cutting to a commercial, you heard her say *"as often as your weather forecasts are."* Such a grimace to see!

Chapter Five

Navigating the Client Relationship

The most important and sacred relationship for the self-employed astrologer is with his client. This covenant and the intimacy that exists between a professional astrologer and his client must never be taken for granted, or underestimated in any way. Life decisions are made as a result of a consultation with you, and it is crucial that you realize the effect your words and attitudes have on your client.

Client relations are governed by the seventh house in astrology, with Saturn as the exalted ruler. Astrologers who have been in practice for many years realize that they become a fixture in the lives of their clients. We are consulted at the birth of children, and are sought after for the times of possible conception for these babies. We weep and are there with our clients when children, parents and spouses die, and we exult with them when that wedding day is planned or that investment pays off.

Astrologers are leaned on for support during that painful divorce, or when the insecurities of a mid-life career change are eroding peace of mind. We listen as clients stagger through spiritual dryness and the absence of hope and optimism. We witness as a client fears necessary surgery, and we are called on to help diagnose medical conditions. We discuss life cycles and time passages in a language of life unparalleled in any of the arts and sciences. We are a friend and a brother or sister.

This relationship is so central to the meaning of our profession that astrologers are ultimately judged only by the quality of service provided to their clientele. If there be one intention set in your heart as you become a self-employed astrologer, let it be love for your clients. They are the primary source of your income, they are the fountain of all your referrals, and they are why you practice in the first place.

In this chapter, I discuss the entire panorama of client relationships: scheduling appointments, preparing for the client, consultation types, fees and payment, the counseling environment, attire and appearance, communication skills, and the decision-making process of the client. Ethical considerations, attitudes of love and service, progressed synastry with clients, appointment charts, consulting with other astrologers, and being a spokesperson for the planets will also be covered.

Scheduling Appointments

The initial contact with any client, whether for a first-time appointment or with a patron that has been with you for many years, should be the basic process of finding out what kind of consultation suits their needs, answering any questions about the nature of your work, and getting them scheduled for an appointment.

When you schedule a client, you are entering into an exchange of fees for service. This type of relationship creates responsibilities for both parties. An astrologer is obligated to adequately prepare for the appointment, and be there at the designated time. The client is held accountable for arriving and paying for this engagement. This must be made quite clear during your initial phone contact.

I keep a telephone log on my desk. Every phone call that I answer, or voice-mail that I listen to, gets recorded in this log. I have dozens of filled-in pads, going back many years, showing every phone call that I have ever received as an astrologer. In this log I record names, birth data, appointment dates and times, addresses and notes of what was discussed with clients as appointments were being scheduled.

From here, I then write this information in my *week AT•A•GLANCE*® model 70-100 appointment book. These spiral-bound, loose-leaf paged appointment books are essential for a self-employed astrologer. This model, which lays flat when opened, shows one week on two adjacent pages. Each day is lined by the half-hour, and I find it very efficient for marking client appointments, the type of consultation scheduled, what date on my phone log has the birth data, etc.

The astrologer will have to practice the balance between being polite and professionally firm over the phone when clients call to schedule appointments. Some, especially when they have had an upset, will launch into their life story while you are trying to get them scheduled. I suggest that you say something to the effect of, *"It is very difficult for me to visualize everything you are saying, and track all of these details, without having the chart in front of me. Please wait until our scheduled consultation so that I can follow your story more closely."* This is a diplomatic way to calm and soothe them.

As a general rule of thumb, the astrologer should spend no more than three to five minutes on the phone when scheduling a client for an appointment. You are being paid to consult with them for a specified fee, on a set date, and for a stated length of time. The client will respect you for discussing only the pertinent information needed to book the appointment.

One thing that the self-employed astrologer must be aware of, especially if they run an ad in the yellow pages and receive calls from the motley public, are individuals who will say they are calling to schedule an appointment, then proceed to milk you for specific interpretations about their chart. Some of these out-of-balance people have no intention to pay you for anything. I have Mercury in Scorpio, and can detect this sort of thing right away, but more guileless astrologers could be taken for a ride.

This type of *caller radar* comes with experience, and seems to be an asset that the

Mercuries in water signs possess to a greater degree than the other elements.

The basic information required to schedule an appointment is:

1) Full name, address and telephone number with area code
2) Date, time and place of birth, plus source of time (birth certificate, mom, etc.)
3) Type of consultation (natal, relationship analysis, progressed, etc.)
4) Date and time of appointment
5) Credit card number and expiration date
6) Brief notes on areas of life to be discussed (career, relationships, etc.)
7) Referred by whom, or where they heard of your practice

You may also find that some clients choose to e-mail you, rather than call you, to schedule their appointments. If they are at work, or desire privacy for any reason, they may prefer to use the Internet. I have had clients e-mail me all of the above information. It is considered professional to return phone calls within one business day, and to reply to e-mails within one or two business days.

Preparing for the Client Appointment

The quality of your consulting work as an astrologer depends to a great extent on the preparation you do for your appointments. I have had many clients come to me who had previously seen another astrologer and were annoyed with their services. The number one complaint was that they perceived the other astrologer to be winging it, meaning it felt like they had just taken the chart out of the computer printer and started interpreting it with no preparation whatsoever. (Don't even think about doing this).

Most competent astrologers are disciplined enough to schedule appropriate lengths of time between appointments for computer chart calculations, chart printing, and preparation notes to be taken. Additionally, astrologers must know their personal limitations and how many clients they can see in a day without a drop in the quality of their work. For some, this is only two sessions per day.

One reason I am all for establishing peer-review groups is that they can be most effective in providing a positive environment in which to perpetuate the professional conduct of astrologers. If one astrologer hears of a disappointing experience a client had with another astrologer, the issue can be brought forward in a safe and supportive atmosphere. If nothing is done, these negative experiences will happen again, continuously dragging down the reputation of astrology itself.

Different types of consultations require different methods of preparation. The most labor intensive are relationship analysis appointments. For these, an astrologer has to review two natal charts, both sets of progressions and transits, synastry aspects, house overlays and the composite chart. Later in this chapter, I will talk about charging higher fees for relationship work.

Preparing for a natal interpretation is pretty straightforward, and these consults may also include vocational analysis, life purpose discussion, and karmic factors. *Chart Interpretation Handbook* by Stephen Arroyo, *The Art of Chart Interpretation* by Tracy Marks, and *The Principles of Astrology* by Charles E.O. Carter are, in my opinion, the most intelligent books around that present step-by-step methods for extracting the essential features from a natal horoscope.

If you are preparing for a transits and progressions consultation, I recommend my book, *Volume I—Progressions,* which has a consultation preparation checklist. I included in that book my techniques for finding the most relevant planetary activity for any point in the client's life. The methods I use include the progressed lunation cycle, the progressed angles, progressed retrogradation, stations, progressed aspects, transits to progressed planets and angles, Sabian symbols, and the transit cycles of Mars, Jupiter and Saturn.

Your preparation for an electional astrology appointment can vary widely, based on the specific needs of your client. I have elected charts for weddings, surgery, the date to incorporate a business, conception dates for couples wishing to have a child, and other cases, many of which were quite unusual. I have workshop tapes on Electional Astrology (see Appendix II).

Besides calculating and printing charts for a client, and technical preparations, there is another dimension of readying oneself for the client appointment. This involves your inner condition, your ability to be present, compassionate and loving during the consultation. This is not always as easy as it sounds.

Astrologers are human beings, and are subject to moods, mental agitation, upsets in life, and other disturbing factors. Peace of mind, intuition and concentration are essential for quality astrological consulting. What can the astrologer do to center himself before the client arrives?

The single most important factor, in my experience, is not to have to rush to get ready. This means that you will have to discipline yourself to stop what you are doing well in advance of the scheduled appointment time and begin to prepare. The astrologer will have to determine just how much time he needs to calculate charts, print them, take notes, get his taping equipment ready, along with being sure to have eaten, groomed and tidied the space before the client walks in the door.

I recommend some form of spiritual balancing or meditation to further prepare for your clients. Personally, I pray and ask to be guided to be able to help this person with their life concerns and needs. I want to feel connected with the Divine when I do my astrology work, and this preparation opens my intuition. I take pride in my work, and with a Gemini Midheaven, the twin pillars of my consulting approach are impeccable technique and intuitive understanding.

In-Person, Telephone & By-Mail Consultation

There are three ways to classify sessions with clients. Two are *consulting,* and one is a *reading.* I have heard astrologers use these two terms interchangeably for many years now, and I perceive a distinct difference between them.

When you meet with a client in person, or talk with them over the telephone, this is *consulting;* simply implying that there is a conversation, or dialogue, taking place between the two of you. When you speak into a boombox, and make a tape for a client that you do not have dialogue with, this is a *reading.*

If you are doing the latter with the former, i.e. having a client, in-person, just sitting and listening to you *read* their chart, with no conversation or questions, then you are not consulting. Readings are for psychic fairs, and are the fire-sale products in professional astrology. Other than an occasional tape that a client may purchase as a gift to a relative, readings, in my opinion, should be declined in your practice and replaced with telephone consultations.

One may ask, *"well, what about clients abroad?"* It used to be that long distance phone service had gaps that plagued overseas connections. Now, however, the quality of long distance is quite clear. I have clients in South Africa, Europe and other places abroad with whom I do successful tape-recorded phone consultation.

In my practice, I offer one-hour telephone consultations and one and one half-hour in-person consultations. Both types of sessions are recorded on cassette tapes. (In the case of phone consultations, I mail the tape, along with the charts, when we conclude). If a client wants to schedule more time over the phone, such as a 90-minute or two hour appointment, I simply pro-rate my fee.

As I wrote in Chapter Two, I recommend that you acquire a toll-free 800 number for your clients. They will often be calling you from the road, from the home of a relative or friend, or from work, and using a phone other than their own. This is a gesture of customer service by the self-employed astrologer to show his love for his clients, and provides a tremendous convenience for them.

Most long distance plans with a calling card charge about 30¢ a minute to use these travel cards, and your 800 number will only cost you about 8¢ a minute from out of state. It makes more sense to add $5 to your consultation fee per hour and absorb the long distance charges, than to have your client get dinged $18 for an hour phone call from the road. Also, clients with cell phones that have high per minute rates can usually find a land line to call from.

Requisite Equipment for Taping Consultations

For both your in-person and telephone consultations, I recommend that you tape the appointment for your client. The reasons for doing this are simple: 1) you will use more discernment in what you say; 2) the client will retain only 20%, at best, of what he hears; and 3) clients will listen to this tape over and over again, each time gleaning more and more of the subtleties of your consultation.

The language of astrology speaks to an individual at the soul level, as it addresses symbol and archetype in the client's life. There is no way that a client can possibly absorb the depth of what you are saying when they initially hear it. Your consultation will reverberate in their heart, mind, body and soul for weeks afterward. Listening to the tape, a client can more fully integrate a session.

There is specific recording equipment necessary to be a self-employed astrologer. For your in-person taping of appointments, you will need a *cassette recorder with an external microphone jack,* along with a *lapel microphone.* Radio Shack makes a nice compact recorder, which is great for travel, model 14-1127, selling for $39.99.

As I will write about later in Chapter Six regarding selling class tapes, they also make an *ultra-miniature tie-clip microphone,* model 33-3013, which sells for $24.99, and comes with a 4 1/2 foot cord. There is a battery unit included, and it has an on-off switch that you *must remember to turn off when not in use.*

For your telephone consultations, you will need a *handset recording controller,* Radio Shack model 43-1237, which sells for $14.99. This device has a phone cord on it that plugs into a modular phone jack, and a secondary cord that plugs into the external microphone jack of your cassette recorder. It records both ends of a phone call, and all you have to do when you have it properly hooked up is to depress both the *play* and *record* buttons on your cassette recorder.

Finally, you will also need to buy blank tapes and get a *duplex adapter,* found at Radio Shack for $4.99. This plastic gizmo plugs into a modular phone jack on your wall, and then allows two phone cords to be plugged into it, *the one for your telephone* and *the one for your recording controller.* Office Depot has 6-packs of blank 60-minute cassette tapes, Maxell UR 60 Normal Bias, which sell for $3.79 a pack. Now, you are ready to consult and tape!

Fee Structure, Sliding Scales & Fee Increases

When you begin your practice, you will need to establish a fee structure. How much you will charge for consultations must be clearly and plainly stated in your marketing literature, such as brochures, flyers and newsletters. You may have potential clients calling your office who cannot afford your fees, and I suggest you have three options ready to offer them.

The first is to sell them a computerized report. I offer these natal, relationship and transit forecasts for $25 each, and they are a lower cost option for a client on a tight budget. Secondly, you can find out how much other local astrologers are charging, and refer clients that cannot afford your fees to a colleague who charges less than you do. Thirdly, you can offer a sliding-scale fee structure.

I have not offered this third option for over ten years because I found that people were constantly abusing my generosity. Anyone who can go out and pay $75 to get their hair cut, or go to dinner, drink some wine, and see a movie for a $50 evening, surely can afford to pay my fees. I recommend offering a sliding scale only to the elderly, single mothers and students.

Presently, I charge $105 per hour for my telephone consultations, and $125 for my in-person appointments, which last 90 minutes (except when I am traveling, in which case these are 60 minutes). I started out in 1989 charging $65 for my consultations. I am now in my 13th year of business and have raised my fees in $10 increments to their present level. This is a fee increase, on average, about every two years. I am told that I am one of the best bargains in the country! (My Pisces Moon?)

I charge $150 for relationship analysis, whether in-person or over the telephone. These appointments require more preparation, with two natal charts involved, the synastry aspects, the house overlays, the composite chart, plus the progressions and transits of both individuals. Sometimes clients will ask you to briefly look at an additional chart during the course of a consultation. A practical policy to implement here is to charge an extra $15 for each further horoscope requested.

Several factors may affect your fee structure. Consider your years of professional experience, as well as your name recognition as an author or as a teaching astrologer in your hometown.

Demographics play into the fee formula as well. A professional astrologer in New York City, with an expensive office in midtown Manhattan, has a substantially higher overhead than, say, an astrologer in Omaha, Nebraska. Wherever the cost of living is higher, astrologer's fees will be higher, as well.

One financial rule in business is that you can take your existing customer base, raise your prices, and increase revenues without finding any new customers. To show how this works for an astrologer, I will give an example. In 2001, I earned $23,148 in consultation fees, out of a total gross income of $48,021. My practice is over 90% telephone consultation, so let's use my $105 per hour rate.

If I raised my telephone consultation fee from $105 to $115 per hour, that would be an increase of about 9.5%. Without adding a single new client, and assuming that my business level would remain the same in 2002, I could earn $2199 more in consultation income by raising my fees (23,148 x 9.5% = 2199). This is equivalent to adding 21 new clients for an initial telephone consultation (105 x 21 = 2205).

Payment of Consultation Fees

Of course, getting paid for your work is crucial. No self-employed astrologer ever wants to be a bill collector, but the reality is that not all clients are as financially responsible as others. I consider myself extremely fortunate to have had a minimum of problems in this area during my career.

I have my natal Moon trine Venus, from the sixth to the second house, with Venus ruling the second and my Moon ruling my eleventh house of income derived from one's business. This is the Cadillac of all aspects for good relationships with customers. I have only had two or three NSF checks written to me in 13 years.

As I wrote in Chapter Three, I have a *merchant services account* and can accept VISA or MasterCard for payment of my consultation fees. This becomes even more important when you have a greater percentage of your clientele from out of state. In the early years of my practice, when I did mostly in-person consultations, my clients paid me by check or with cash. I rarely ever invoiced anybody.

As I developed my astrological mail-order business, selling charts, reports, tapes, calendars and books through the mail, I began to accept telephone orders without prepayment, and sent a sales order invoice along with the shipments. Most customers were very responsible about mailing me a check within 30 days. If they did not, I phoned, politely but firmly reminding them that the invoice was past-due.

The smartest business move I ever made as an astrologer was to get that merchant services account. My regular clients pay by credit card on the day of the telephone consultation appointment, and I keep their card numbers and expiration dates in my data base. I require new clients to hold their initial appointment booking with a credit card, and I run the transaction through my electronic terminal to make sure that the card is good *before* I begin my consultation preparation work.

If you are just beginning your practice, I have some advice for you. Don't start invoicing clients, but insist on payment the day of the appointment. Cash flow is a huge problem for an astrologer, and employed people just don't quite understand what it is like to live without a paycheck. When a client pays by credit card, the money is deposited electronically into your business checking account that day.

Occasionally, a client will have a legitimate bad luck story about why they really need a consultation, but cannot pay all of your fee, and they do not use plastic. I am not so much of a hardened Scorpio that my softer Pisces Moon cannot be appealed to. In these circumstances, I recommend that you go ahead and charge them 50% of your fee on the day of the appointment, and bill them for the balance.

Your Professional Consultation Environment

An important aspect of customer service, as an astrologer, is to help your client feel as comfortable as possible during a consultation. This is more than a cushy upholstered chair to sit in, and a cup of tea to offer them. Your office, and in particular its cleanliness, will have a strong impact on your client's experience.

Cat hair from the sweater of the last client left on the chair looks and feels funky, and little things like brushing it off before the next appointment, or vacuuming the carpet for that clean look, are significant for the comfort of your client. Having your desk tidy and organized, your bookshelf straight and orderly, and no piles of junk on the floor are small ways to express respect for your client.

If you have a consultation with a client who is emotionally agitated, or grieving over the death or loss of a loved one, the astrologer should clear the room before the next client comes in. This can be done by smudging, opening a window, praying to raise up the pain and sorrow to God's care, or burning a scented candle.

Many clients who come to see astrologers are highly sensitive souls, and absorb a lot of the energetic vibrations in the environment around them. You can create a better atmosphere for yourself and your client by being sensitive to these factors. If you are feeling overwhelmed by the intensity of your last client, you owe it to the next one to go outside and take a walk to get some fresh air.

How your office is decorated, the warmth of your furniture, and the welcome that you give your client when they walk through the door are all intangible, yet very important ingredients that contribute to the overall consultation experience. I offer my clients a hug when they come and before they go, and I have a picture of Jesus on the wall to help create an atmosphere of love, forgiveness and peace. It is the demeanor and character of the astrologer himself which the client most notices.

Attire & Appearance

I am the kind of person who is not really that big on clothing, as my Venus-Saturn conjunction is rather utilitarian when it comes to personal fashion. Plus, I have lived in the Pacific Northwest for many years, where casual dress is the rule. My clients have all seen me in blue jeans and a polo shirt through the years, and now, doing phone consultations from my home office, I am often in my house slippers and a tee shirt. In person, though, your attire should match your clientele's.

If you have leased commercial office space in a professional building, I would recommend that your dress up a little to fit in with your neighbors. If you have a largely corporate clientele, with individuals arriving at your office dressed in suits, then it is a professional courtesy to try to match your attire with theirs.

The point is, regardless of the sort of clothing you prefer, it's best to be neat, clean and groomed. Even though I look like a bohemian, when I see a client, my teeth are brushed, my beard is trimmed, and my shirt is tucked in. I have had clients in my office who had enough jewelry on to pay my rent for four years (usually Leos or Tauruses with Pisces rising!), and I have had clients who looked like they shop at thrift stores. I don't really pay attention to how people dress, but others do, and the astrologer should at least be somewhat conscious of the initial impression that he makes with his appearance.

There is a subculture within the world of astrology who look like a crowd coming from a Grateful Dead concert, wearing headscarves, colorful costumes, and oils that smell like an opium den in Morocco. I don't mind clients who look like extras in a Woodstock film, but, in my opinion, astrologers shouldn't. We have enough of an image problem already.

Communication Skills

The relationship between the successful self-employed astrologer and his client requires well-developed communication skills. I have observed many of my best students feeling intimidated about beginning a practice of astrology because they felt unable to fully articulate what they saw in the birthchart. A process of translation must occur, transforming the planetary symbolism into the language of everyday human experience.

It stands to reason, then, that the confidence which a student of astrology has in his communication skills will affect his ability to practice. Planets in Gemini or Virgo, or in the third or sixth houses, Mercury sextile or trine to the Ascendant, and other helpful horoscope factors, may give an astrologer natural relating abilities. For those who do not possess these kinds of birthcharts, some effort will be necessary to develop their competence as a communicator.

Many modern-day astrologers are also psychotherapists, and have been trained at the university level in listening skills, observational perception, empathy and other interpersonal techniques. It can be useful for a newly self-employed astrologer to take a class at a community college in counseling skills. There are also several books in print about these techniques.

Another factor in helping astrologers improve communications with clients is a simple interest in their well-being. When I first began to practice, I had an agenda that I thought should be covered during the consultation, one which included everything written down in my preparation notes. Over the years, I have come to realize that sometimes a client will have only one burning issue that they need to talk about. My ability to listen and hear this is crucial.

When the astrologer prepares for a consultation, he will list several aspects that he sees forming in the progressions and transits, and may also notice similar planets in the solar return chart being aspected. If, for example, a client is having progressed Venus aspecting natal Neptune, transiting Neptune aspecting their natal seventh house ruler, and Venus in the solar return chart is also in aspect to Neptune, they may only need to discuss financial fears and relational worries. The art of consulting is in connecting the planets directly to the client's experience.

It is my belief that the astrologer's preparation work goes hand-in-hand with his communication skills used during the consultation. There is a peace of mind that the thoroughly-prepared astrologer radiates to his client, as if he sees from an eagle-eyed vantage point all that is going on in their life. This aura of thorough preparedness, in my view, creates trust and helps in communication.

The Decision-Making Process of the Client

The most sensitive area of your relationship with a client lies in their decision-making process. As an astrologer, you will be leaned on to make judgments based on what you see in the various horoscopes. This is different than making a choice for your client, which should absolutely be avoided and left for them to do. A very fine line exists between providing guidance and making choices for the client.

One way to navigate through these waters is to ask questions such as *what do you think is the right thing to do here?* or *what is your inner voice telling you to do?* The client will have the answer to any difficult question within themselves, and the role of an astrologer is to frame the questions, articulate the choices, and then get out of the way and let the client choose. Silence can be most effective here.

Consultations can easily become quite emotional with crying, laughter, anger, frustration, bitterness or remorse taking place in your office. Through the years, I have learned to open my heart and enter into the feelings of my clients. I have wept with them, I have laughed with them, I have waxed soulful with them, and I have pumped my fist along with their determination to change. All a client may need, sometimes, is just to be heard, and not be judged or shamed.

Some of the most brutal emotional environments I have ever endured were during relationship analysis consultations. The couple may be on the brink of ending a relationship, or, perhaps, about to have a transformational breakthrough and reach a new level of intimacy. Man, you can get pounded during these sessions.

Before I wised up, and positioned the client chairs so that the man and woman were facing each other, not me, I used to get blasted with emotional venom. My Pisces Moon would be dazed after the ninety-minute consultation was finished, and I would have to go drink a beer to take the edge off. I found these sessions to be highly cathartic for the couple, as they would express to each other feelings that previously had been only thoughts. Astrology reaches people at a soul level.

One consultation I will not touch with a ten-foot pole is for a married person who is considering having an affair, and wants you to look at the synastry and composite chart for them and the potential lover. What the client really wants is for you to advise them to leave a relationship, and they want to use the astrology with the third person to rationalize their choice.

I have refused to accept this type of appointment, and I have had people curse me over the phone for being righteous and opprobrious. Rather that, I said, than the bad karma of justifying infidelity with astrological rationale. Additionally, it is an ethical requirement for the astrologer to inquire whether or not a person has permission from another to use secondary birth data during a consultation.

Ethical Considerations

As I wrote in earlier chapters, some of the national organizations, such as *ISAR* and *NCGR*, have started ethics training seminars for astrologers. This has raised quite a stink, with contentious dialogue flying back and forth between the two opposing viewpoints. In a nutshell, *the therapist model* for an astrology practice versus *the independent consultant model* are at odds here.

The therapist model views an astrologer as a counselor, intimately involved in the emotional and psychological process of the client, with a specific arena of ethical concerns similar to a psychotherapist-client relationship. On the other hand, the independent consultant model views the astrologer almost as a celestial attorney, advising the client on planetary strategies, yet remaining out of the soup of the client's emotional life, with a more objective and analytical approach.

I, myself, feel comfortable in a third classification, one of a metaphysical priest or medicine man, if you will. In this model, the astrologer, using the symbols and archetypes, enters into an altered state with a client, and essentially communicates what the relevant planetary forces are revealing. This model encompasses both the emotional intimacy of the therapist and the analysis of the independent consultant.

In my opinion, every astrologer ought to be held responsible to his clients for the soundness and common sense of his guidance. These ethical concerns are partially regulated by market laws of supply and demand. If a client has a bad consultation with an astrologer, they will not return again; and the subsequent astrologer that hears about it will not refer to that astrologer, thus resulting in natural controls.

Many of the various ethical concerns for astrologers, such as sexual relations with clients, scare tactics in marketing, confidentiality, interfering with the choice-making responsibilities of the client, and improper fees and charges are well detailed in some of the literature that *ISAR* and *NCGR* have published so far.

Another group that addresses ethical issues is *The Organization for Professional Astrology.* In *How to Start, Maintain and Expand an Astrological Practice* (in which I contributed a chapter on *Teaching Astrology & Becoming A Self-Published Astrological Author),* there is a summary of *ISAR's* ethics seminar (written by David Cochrane).

When I attended the seminar at the *ISAR 2000* conference in Anaheim, California, as part of the first group of astrologers who received *C.A.P.* honors *(Certified Astrology Professional),* I did not hear a single reference in the context of ethics, made to the spiritual dimension of the astrologer-client relationship. For me, this is crucial to proper behavior by an astrologer and is at the core of my work.

Working With an Attitude of Love & Service

I believe that the relationship between an astrologer and client is a sacred one, and if the intention is set in the heart of the astrologer to love and serve his clients, then how could he go wrong? One way to visualize this is by contemplating the ninth house, which rules morals, principles and ethics. The eighth house, which has a twelfth house relationship to the ninth through the derivative house system, would then represent the spiritual protection of, or the undoing of, ethical work.

This eighth house, at its worst, reveals how some unethical astrologers may use emotionally subversive tactics, such as fear, manipulation and control, to wrongly influence a client, or to keep a client returning in an unhealthy dependency on the astrologer. This is just plain wrong, in all cases.

On the other hand, an astrologer working through positive eighth house energies, can offer himself, through an attitude of love and service, as a transformational vehicle for the client to merge with, through the symbolic dialogue that takes place within a consultation. Such an offering can spiritually protect both his client and his work.

I have had this experience repeatedly in my practice, one which I can only describe as a very intimate feeling of having gone into a shamanic, or altered state with my client. Our soul purposes would merge on some subtle level of consciousness. After the appointment was finished, I would have a weary and spent feeling, completely satisfied with knowing I conveyed important archetypal truths and symbolic meaning about their life to them.

Progressed Synastry with the Client

One way to more fully understand the nature of the relationship between you and your client is to investigate your progressed synastry aspects for the day of the consultation. I have quite regularly found that these aspects illustrate the essential purpose of the session; i.e. why the client is seeing you on that day, not two years before, nor three years in the future.

For example, if the client's secondary progressed Ascendant is conjunct your natal Saturn, then the consultation will require you to be the voice of restraint, an image of discipline, or simply a common sense advocate for decision-making with long term implications. On the other hand, if their progressed Midheaven is conjunct your natal Jupiter or Uranus, you will likely find yourself encouraging your client to make changes or take some risks in his career.

These consultation dynamics will occur whether or not you know the astrological underpinnings for them, so you do not have to worry about prejudicing your approach by researching the progressed synastry. The astrologer may also find that the degree of his current secondary progressed Moon or Sun will be the degree of a client's natal Ascendant, MC or either of the Lights.

I feel there is a life force transfusion taking place between the astrologer and client, and the synastric progressions facilitate this occurrence. I have always felt awe and wonderment toward the mystery of the spirit world, and it is my belief that the degrees of progressed conjunctions, in synastry, reflect the timing of the connection between astrologer and client.

The Consultation Appointment Chart

Still another method for comprehending the connection between the astrologer and his client is to cast the chart for the date and time of the consultation. This chart reflects a moment in time, as a horary chart, and the outcome of the consult can be seen within it. An astrologer can glean valuable insight from this.

For example, if a mother schedules an appointment to discuss her sixteen year old son's horoscope, and on that day, and at that time, the Moon is exactly square the lunar nodes, the astrologer may presume that the consultation would affect the way that she perceives the boy's future and his purpose in life. If Venus be sextile to Mars on that day as well, then the son's interest in girls will come up.

If the astrologer finds that there is a void-of-course Moon at the time of an appointment, then he can assume that no definite decision will emerge, and that the session will be mostly about perspective and a review of life cycles. If the client comes in on the day of their lunar return, then the astrologer may presume that a new course in life is about to begin. These charts are highly informative, and only take a few minutes to view.

Consulting to Other Astrologers

As I wrote in Chapter One, I have had many astrologers schedule consultations with me. Some were doing this to observe my techniques, find out what my fees were, see my office or how I ran my practice. Others were in actual need of some help as they were going through difficult passages in their lives. Either way, I have always been known as an astrologer's astrologer, and I take pride in this.

I have noticed that the term *astrologer* has many different gradations of meaning. Those who call themselves astrologers may be *hobbyists, amateurs, students, part-time professionals,* or *full-time professionals.*

When I first joined the board of the Oregon Astrological Association in 1991, I set out to create a practicing astrologer's directory. In the questionnaire that was sent to the membership, these above five categories were listed for individuals to describe their level of astrological study or practice. Apparently, many had never been asked this before, and resented it, based on the responses given.

Anyone who purchases an astrology software program, prints up some business cards, and knows Taurus from Sagittarius can call themselves an astrologer. I was trying to discern the hierarchy that I felt should be relevant amongst students, amateurs and professionals. Perfectly natural for my Capricorn North Node, yet I was somewhat surprised by the resentment generated over the use of these terms.

What I am trying to say here is that there is an unspoken chain of command present in the world of astrology. At the top of the profession are the authors, next come the self-employed, full- time professionals, then the part-time professionals, then amateurs (interpreting horoscopes for no fee), then hobbyists (using astrology on themselves only), and finally the students.

Every astrologer at each level can benefit from the ones above him. This is why, in my opinion, students, hobbyists or part-time professionals will seek out a full-time astrologer for a consultation. On some level, they perhaps know that *you can only really call yourself an astrologer when you devote your whole being to it, and solely derive your income from astrological work alone.* Thus, some transfer of love for the profession occurs between the dedicated full-time astrologer and the others.

The Sabian Symbol for the 12th degree of Aquarius is: *On A Vast Staircase Stand People Of Different Types, Graduated Upward.* This symbolism speaks to the ideal of humanity, wherein those above extend a hand to those below, while themselves receiving a hand from those above. This philosophical approach to consulting with other astrologers expressly implies that the full-time self-employed ones have a sacred duty to encourage the others, and to serve as a role model for them.

Being a Spokesperson for the Planets

As I conclude this chapter on my thoughts about navigating the relationship with the client, I want to share concepts that I have about my work with you. Because I am Mercury-ruled, both personally and professionally (Virgo ascending and Gemini culminating), I have long identified with the saying, *Don't kill the messenger.*

What I do as an astrologer is simply to speak for the solar system as it affects the lives of my clients. I can see the celestial spheres in geometric relationship with the nativity of the person, and I am articulating these planetary and zodiacal forces as a language of life, translating them into everyday human experience.

I did not personally cause this planetary motion to happen, but I am being paid to define and describe what is occurring in the heavenly realms that affects my client on earth. Thus, I stand in the transitional territory between heaven and earth, as a mediator for the planets and Zodiac to express their energies to the human realm.

If one dwells on this concept for any length of time, it starts to feel rather bizarre, as if an astrologer were some sort of spiritual mutant, neither of this world, nor of the heavenly realms, but living in an in-between place, like a shaman or a medicine man. It is a lonely feeling as an earthly being, and an equally lonely sensation as a spirit, for one is not quite fully an inhabitant of either realm.

This, in my understanding of Mercury, is the existential agony of the messenger. He knows no rest in either world, but strives to provide quietude to those seeking to align their earthly selves with the heavenly realms. It was with this in mind that I visualized the radical new technique for aspect interpretation in *Volume II*.

By overlaying the 360° aspect circle onto the Zodiac circle, and illustrating how the angular separation between planets could define their relationship by using the Sabian Symbol for this degree, I wanted to give power back to the Zodiac for all aspect interpretation. Any two heavenly bodies at a specific degree of angular separation would then have the same symbolic relationship.

Since the 1970's, too much emphasis has been given to the planetary archetypes, and not enough to the spiritual power contained within the living forces of the Zodiac. This is, in large part, due to the ascendancy of psychological astrology, its overemphasis on the planets, and the Pluto in Leo generation's egocentric disproportions. I felt that a radical paradigm shift in our approach to aspects would serve to restore the power of the Zodiac to its rightful place in astrology. This was the underlying intention of *Sabian Aspect Orbs*.

If the astrologer views himself less as a spokesperson for the planets, but knows deep in his heart that the Zodiac is the true living spiritual force and power in astrology, then how he communicates with his client is radically shifted. Never again will the planets be feared, nor will this fear be subconsciously projected onto the client. In my world-view, modern astrologers are over-identified with the planets, and unfortunately disassociated from the living Zodiac.

Chapter Six

Teaching Astrology & Public Speaking

Because clientele income is erratic and unpredictable for all new self-employed astrologers, it is a matter of economic survival to diversify your business so that you can create different sources of revenue. With a Gemini Midheaven and Virgo Ascendant, and their common ruler in my 3rd house, it was quite natural for me to start a school of astrology, a mail-order business, an agency for software sales, and a teaching, writing and lecturing career, all being Mercury-ruled occupations.

I was altogether determined to make it financially as a full-time astrologer, no matter what, and I found that my innate Scorpionic resourcefulness would always kick in when I was up against the wall and broke. None of us go into the profession of astrology just because we want to make money, but the self-employed experience will test your mettle and demand you to be resolute.

In this chapter, I will share my experiences of founding a school of astrology, teaching classes at bookstores, community colleges and metaphysical centers, designing course outlines, creating handouts, offering workshops, attracting students, earning income from tapes, and speaking in public. It is my hope that this educational business model will help you to earn additional astrological income.

How Teaching Contributes Income to Your Practice

My experience has shown me that when you are building an astrological practice, teaching beginning astrology classes is the engine that pulls the entire income train down the tracks. Beginning students become regular clients, buy astrology software, books, tapes, charts and reports from you, refer family and friends to your practice, go on to take intermediate and advanced classes, attend your lectures and workshops, and remain a part of your loyal customer base for years.

Teaching astrology will result in some of your students becoming clients. During class time many examples from the student's birth charts will be used to illustrate the material being taught, but the teaching astrologer can't give extended personal attention without disrupting the flow of the class. Some students, therefore, will feel inspired to see you for a consultation.

If you have become an astrological software dealer, you will now find the classroom to be the ideal environment for program sales. Most students will start out buying charts from you of their family members, so that they can look at other horoscopes besides their own as they are learning. Toward the middle of my eight-week beginning class, I could tell who the motivated students were, and who were most likely to acquire software.

Later in this chapter, I will discuss how you can create a little bookstore for your students, making a small profit for your business. We will also discuss taping your classes, as these can be sold locally and by mail-order.

Where are the Teaching Opportunities?

I have taught beginning astrology classes at community colleges, metaphysical centers, local Theosophical Society chapters, New Thought churches, several different bookstores, and at my former school in Portland, Oregon. I have taught classes with as few as three students, and with as many as twenty-five to fifty at community colleges and at the Theosophical Society.

Last year I was invited to join the faculty of the ONLINE College of Astrology, an Internet astrology school with AOL-style chat rooms (classrooms) where the students and instructor meet weekly for question and answer sessions; students do homework, reading assignments and chart analysis projects between classes.

As previously mentioned, the astrologer with a newly established practice finds out in a hurry how erratic clientele income can be. The wear and tear on the astrologer's nervous system from his concerns over fluctuating monthly income may affect the functioning of his intellect and intuition during consultations.

As I wrote in Chapter Four on *Marketing and Advertising,* display ads can never accomplish what referrals will. The repetition required for any ad to produce consistent new customer contact can take as long as three years. For referrals to occur, the astrologer has to take himself to the potential customer base, rather than wait for clients to come to him through advertising—so, get out there and teach!

Starting a School of Astrology

You are more likely to get invited to teach at an outside venue if you already have a school of astrology. This is not as difficult to start as it may sound. If you have leased commercial office space for consultations, you can hold classes there as well. With some stacking or folding chairs that can be stored in a closet, a white board and some colored dry-erase markers, you are ready to roll.

I also recommend purchasing a *Cram's Imperial World Globe* for your classroom, which can be found inexpensively at *Toys 'R' Us.* These handy globes include the ecliptic, showing where it intersects the equator twice at the Greenwich meridian and the international date line, and even have the degrees of the Zodiac shown! You know that *a picture is worth 1000 words,* and the astronomy of astrology can be taught so much more easily with this educational prop in your classroom.

Most leases for office space simply state that the suite is to be used for commercial purposes; client consulting and teaching both fall safely into this classification. I have taught evening classes two or three times a week for many years, and most tenants in the building were long gone by the time class began at 7:00 PM. For your protection, with or without lease requirements, I suggest that you get business insurance. This covers liability of two million dollars, and costs ± $150 a year.

If you have taken out a box ad in your local yellow pages under *Astrologers,* you will receive a complimentary listing. You can place it under the *Schools* heading in the directory, thus giving you dual exposure for your business.

You can start a bookstore as part of your school, and I recommend your beginning class textbook to be *Chart Interpretation Handbook* by Stephen Arroyo. To receive a 40% discount off of the cover price (you pay shipping), and be able to make a small profit selling books, you can call CRCS Publications in Sebastopol, California, at 707.829.0735 (publisher of Mr. Arroyo's books), to set up a wholesale account.

If you intend to teach regularly, it would be wise to bring in a few other titles from CRCS written by Mr. Arroyo, Bil Tierney, Tracy Marks or Liz Greene to expand the selection of books in your classroom. Don't forget to charge and report state sales tax for books. (Tax is not required for student tuition payments).

Teaching at Bookstores, Community Colleges & Metaphysical Centers

Wherever you live, there are teaching opportunities for the resourceful astrologer. You can approach your local bookstores, community college continuing education departments, metaphysical centers, psychic institutes, New Thought churches, coffee houses, New Age gift stores, or any other venue that you feel would have an interest in offering a class. Many store owners are looking for ways to get more customers into their emporium, and classes are the perfect match for this.

I taught beginning astrology classes at Portland Community College in 1991-1992. I called the adult education division about a class proposal, then scheduled an interview with a department manager, and was hired as a part-time instructor. The college advertised the class in their catalogue, handled all of the registration, and assigned me to a classroom in a local high school for the evenings.

The first class had a great turnout with about 25 students enrolling. I taught it the following quarter, again with over 20 students. The college then received a letter from a fundamentalist imbecile complaining about *pseudo-scientific curriculum,* and my class was abruptly canceled, effective at the quarter's end. Transit Jupiter in Virgo, ruling higher education, was in my 12th house and I got blindsided!

A letter-writing campaign was launched by my students to reinstate the class, and 90 letters were sent to the college president addressing issues of academic freedom, but the spineless fool would not relent. In fact, the college then went on a witch hunt, removing every class in the adult education curriculum that taught yoga, psychic development, meditation, tarot and anything else metaphysical.

Transit Pluto was conjunct my Sun then, and this experience along with my frustrations at the bookstore, where I was also teaching as their in-house astrologer, led me to take the bull by the horns and start my own school of astrology. Did somebody say that Pluto rules power and control issues?

While I was teaching classes at my school, I also approached bookstores in the community about offering classes. My colleague, Virginia Dayan, who owned the *Dragon's Head* bookstore in SE Portland, hired me to teach an advanced chart interpretation class one night a week.

A New Thought church, *Living Enrichment Center,* with a huge congregation of over 2000, also hired me to teach a class there. There was also a metaphysical church in Salem that later invited me to teach beginning and intermediate classes.

If you have a local chapter of the Theosophical Society in your city, they may have a Sunday afternoon free public lecture program. In Portland, I was invited by the chapter to give a series of seven classes on Esoteric Astrology which were attended by large crowds, some lectures drawing well over 50 people.

My income from teaching locally, both at my own school and at other venues in Portland, was as high as $3900 in class tuition during 1993-4, and $2650 in workshop tuition during 1995. This combined income represented about 1/6 to 1/8 of my overall gross. The resulting earnings in other areas of my astrology business, i.e. consultations, software sales, books, tapes, reports, etc., derived from these students is hard to precisely estimate, but was a significant contribution to my gross income each year.

Designing a Beginning Class Syllabus

Whether you start a school of astrology or just teach at local bookstores, you will need to design a course outline. I recommend that your beginning class be no longer than eight weeks, the maximum length of a new student's attention span and sustained interest. A six-week class can be adequate, but not as comprehensive.

The following is the outline for the beginning course that I have taught for years:

Week 1: Elements, Modes & Zodiac Signs
Week 2: The Planets
Week 3: The Houses
Week 4: Aspects I
Week 5: Aspects II
Week 6: Planetary Patterns & Aspect Configurations
Week 7: Chart Synthesis

Week 8: Student Chart Examples

A more detailed beginning class syllabus is included next for your reference:

WEEK ONE

A) Introductions - Intent of Class
B) The Elements - Fire • Earth • Air • Water
C) The Qualities - Cardinal • Fixed • Mutable
D) The Twelve Signs • The Zodiac
E) Questions and Answers

WEEK TWO

A) The Solar System Model of Planetary Consciousness
B) The Personal Planets
    1) The Sun 2) The Moon 3) Mercury 4) Venus 5) Mars
C) The Social Planets
    1) Jupiter 2) Saturn
D) The Transformational/Generational Planets
    1) Uranus 2) Neptune 3) Pluto
E) Questions and Answers

WEEK THREE

A) The Construction of the Horoscope
    1) The Horizon 2) The Meridian 3) The Equator 4) The Ecliptic
    5) The Zodiac 6) The Intersection of the Ecliptic and the Equator
    7) The Four Birthchart Angles
    a) The Ascendant b) The Nadir c) The Descendant d) The Midheaven
B) The Hemispheres
C) The Quadrants
D) The Twelve Houses
    1) The Angular Houses - 1 • 4 • 7 • 10
    2) The Succedent Houses - 2 • 5 • 8 • 11
    3) The Cadent Houses - 3 • 6 • 9 • 12
    4) The Fire Houses - 1 • 5 • 9
    5) The Earth Houses - 2 • 6 • 10
    6) The Air Houses - 3 • 7 • 11
    7) The Water Houses - 4 • 8 • 12
E) Rising Signs
F) Questions and Answers

WEEK FOUR

A) The Astrological Alphabet: Letters 1 through 12
B) Aspects as Planetary Relationships
    1) Planetary Dynamics & Protocol 2) Aspects to the Sun

3) Aspects to the Moon	4) Aspects to Mercury
5) Aspects to Venus	6) Aspects to Mars
7) Aspects to Jupiter	8) Aspects to Saturn
9) Aspects to Uranus	10) Aspects to Neptune
11) Aspects to Pluto	12) Aspects to the Ascendant & MC

C) The Major Aspects • Part I
      1) Conjunction 2) Opposition 3) Trine 4) Square
D) Unaspected Planets
E) Sign & House Placements
F) Questions and Answers

WEEK FIVE
A) The 360° Holistic Cycle Concept
B) The Major Aspects • Part II
      1) Conjunction 2) Opposition 3) Trine 4) Square
C) The Minor Aspects
      1) Semisextile 2) Semisquare 3) Sextile 4) Sesquiquadrate 5) Quincunx
D) The Esoteric Aspects
      1) Quintile 2) Septile 3) Novile 4) Decile 5) Undecile
E) Finding Aspects in Birthcharts
F) Sign & House Placements
G) Questions and Answers

WEEK SIX
A) The Birth Chart As A Whole
B) Planetary Patterns

1) Splash	5) Seesaw
2) Bowl	6) Bundle
3) Bucket	7) Fan
4) Locomotive	8) Splay

C) Aspect Configurations

1) Stellium	5) T-Square
2) Grand Trine	6) Grand Cross
3) Kite	7) Mystic Rectangle
4) Yod	8) Grand Sextile

D) Questions and Answers

WEEK SEVEN
A) Preponderances and Deficiencies

1) By Element	2) By Quality
3) By Hemisphere	4) By Quadrant

B) Chart Ruler (Planetary Ruler of the Ascendant)
C) Planetary Ruler of the Midheaven

D) Horoscope Synthesis - Putting It All Together

E) Planets in Signs

F) Planets in Signs in Houses

G) Planets in Signs in Houses in Aspect

H) House Rulerships and Dispositors

I) Sun - Moon Phases

1) New ●	5) Full ○
2) Crescent ☽	6) Disseminating ◖
3) First Quarter ◐	7) Third Quarter ◑
4) Gibbous ◗	8) Balsamic ☾

J) Questions and Answers

WEEK EIGHT

A) Student Birth Chart Examples

B) Speaking the Astrological Language

C) Responsibilities and Obligations in Using Astrology

With a detailed beginning course outline such as this, professionally bound in a report cover with your business card attached, you can confidently stride into any bookstore and meet with the owner to discuss teaching at their establishment. As mentioned in Chapter Four in the section on *Circulating Brochures & Business Cards,* it will be better for you to make phone contact initially before going in.

Textbooks, Weekly Handouts & Homework Assignments

To teach a beginning astrology class thoroughly and efficiently, you will need to provide handouts to your students each week and give them homework along with a reading assignment. As stated earlier, I recommend your beginning class textbook to be *Chart Interpretation Handbook* by Stephen Arroyo [CRCS Publications; 1989].

I have found this book to be very well received by students It is concisely and intelligently written, with psychological insight about planetary, sign, house and aspect meanings. There are chapters in the book where students can read personal interpretations for their planets in signs, their Ascendant, and their natal aspects.

I have always provided my students with weekly handouts, which were expanded versions of my detailed class outline shown earlier in this chapter. To keep the attention of your students while teaching requires the engagement of two of their senses, namely sight and hearing, and this is why handouts, along with charts and notes on your whiteboard, are essential for an orderly classroom experience.

My homework assignments consist of reading from the textbook and written essays each week. I will list the recommended reading and papers for you:

[all reading assignments from *Chart Interpretation Handbook*]

Night of Week One READING ASSIGNMENT FOR WEEK TWO: Pages 1 - 34 (Chapters 1-3 + Introduction)

HOMEWORK ASSIGNMENT FOR WEEK TWO: Write a short essay about how you see the fire, earth, air and water elements in action; by either observing other people or nature, or through your interaction with others and/or nature.

Night of Week Two READING ASSIGNMENT FOR WEEK THREE: Pages 35 - 90 (Chapters 4-5). Please find the specific birth chart interpretations for your natal planets in their signs in chapter 5.

HOMEWORK ASSIGNMENT FOR WEEK THREE: Write a short essay about how you perceive the layers of planetary consciousness as concentric circles surrounding your Spirit/Heart. With the Sun at the center, describe your: mental layer/perceptions • feelings/senses • past/Soul/emotions • desires/will • self-improvement • lessons of experience • urge to individuate • loss of self • renewal of self. You may use personal examples to illustrate your conceptual reasoning.

Night of Week Three READING ASSIGNMENT FOR WEEK FOUR: Pages 91-130 (Chapters 6-7).

HOMEWORK ASSIGNMENT FOR WEEK FOUR: Draw in the glyphs of the signs that are on your house cusps on the blank chart wheel provided. Then, draw in the glyphs for your planets, placing them in the appropriate houses. Next, write a short essay about the houses your Sun and Moon are in, and explain how you see those external environments as active in your daily life. Then describe your ascendant, and how you frame the world looking out through your eyes.

Night of Week Four READING ASSIGNMENT FOR WEEK FIVE: Pages 131-167 (Chapter 8). Look up the interpretations for each of your planetary aspects.

HOMEWORK ASSIGNMENT FOR WEEK FIVE: Make a list of all your natal planetary aspects and orb of exactitude. Start with the Sun and work your way out to Pluto. Include aspects to your Ascendant and Midheaven.

Night of Week Five 1st HOMEWORK ASSIGNMENT FOR WEEK SIX: List the conjunctions, squares, trines and oppositions in your instructor's chart below.

2nd HOMEWORK ASSIGNMENT FOR WEEK SIX: List all your astrological alphabet combinations in four columns: 1) Planets in signs; 2) Planets in houses; 3) Signs on house cusps; 4) Planetary aspects. Make a note of any two-letter themes repeating three or more times.

Night of Week Six READING ASSIGNMENT FOR WEEK SEVEN: Pages 169-181 (Chapter 9).

HOMEWORK ASSIGNMENT FOR WEEK SEVEN: Assess your birth chart for planetary patterns and aspect configurations.

<u>Night of Week Seven</u> READING ASSIGNMENT FOR WEEK EIGHT: Reread Chapter 8 (Aspects).

HOMEWORK ASSIGNMENT FOR WEEK EIGHT: Write a short essay describing any preponderances or deficiencies you may have, and how you experience them. Find the planetary rulers of your Ascendant and Midheaven, and write a short essay analyzing them by sign, house and aspect.

Tuition Fees & Pre-Registration Incentives

I have charged from $90 to $300 for my classes, depending on length (8 or 12 weeks) and whether I was paid the tuition directly, or if a percentage was kept by the facility where I was teaching. I feel that $15 per class per student is fair. Thus an eight-week class with a compensation to the astrologer of $120 per student should be par for the course in most cities in the U.S. and Canada.

If you are teaching through a bookstore, where they keep a percentage, you will have to increase the tuition in order to net this amount for yourself. If you wind up teaching at venues other than your school, you will learn the art of negotiation. It is not fair for the bookstore owner or metaphysical center to keep more than 30% of the gross tuition revenues, meaning that you need to receive 70¢ of each dollar.

In my opinion, it is better to walk away from a teaching gig where the bookstore owner wants to keep 50% of the tuition, than to cower and compromise your dignity. The only exception to this should be teaching on the Internet, where the school owner has enormous costs to keep the website running, and can only pay the instructor 50% of the gross tuition earned.

I have negotiated teaching contracts in which I collected the tuition and repaid the store in a graduated scale; 4-6 students enrolled = 15% of gross; 7-9 students = 20%; 10-12 students = 25%, etc. Thus, the bookstore has an incentive to promote.

If you start your own school of astrology, you will be responsible for collecting tuition from the students. Early enrollment saves you from last-minute headaches, and to get your students to pre-register well in advance of the start of class, you can mail out a registration form that will be returned with a check or credit card number. Some teaching astrologers will offer incentives, such as tuition discounts to students who register before a stated deadline.

Designing an Intermediate Class Syllabus

About four of every ten beginning students will want to go on to an intermediate class. Taking pupils past the foundations of the astrological language requires an immersion into technique, so that they can integrate concepts with application. To now hold a student's interest, the instructor has to teach methods.

Ideally, your intermediate class should only be scheduled every other quarter, thus allowing the graduated beginners to accumulate, to ensure better registration for this class. I would recommend teaching the beginning class year-round, offering it four quarters a year. The Fall quarter should end before Thanksgiving, and the Winter quarter should begin after New Year's to avoid conflict with the Holidays.

I recommend the following eight-week course outline for your next class level:

> Week 1: Retrograde Planets
> Week 2: Transits
> Week 3: Progressions
> Week 4: Lunar Nodes & Life Purpose
> Week 5: Relationship Analysis Techniques
> Week 6: Aspects & 360° Cycle Analysis
> Week 7: Solar Returns
> Week 8: House Rulerships & Dispositors

As I did with my beginning class, I prepared detailed handouts for my students in the intermediate class. I included a recommended reading list for the technique that was being taught each week. I will list these books for you here:

Week One on Retrograde Planets

> *Retrogrades* by Mohan Koparkar, Ph.D.
> *Dynamics Of Aspect Analysis* by Bil Tierney
> *Your Hidden Powers* by Joanne Wickenburg
> *The Art Of Chart Interpretation* by Tracy Marks
> *Karmic Astrology-Volume II: Retrogrades & Reincarnation* by Martin Schulman

Week Two on Transits

> *Planets In Transit* by Robert Hand
> *Modern Transits* by Lois M. Rodden
> *The Progressed Horoscope* by Alan Leo
> *Relationships & Life Cycles* by Stephen Arroyo
> *The Principles of Astrology* by Charles E.O. Carter
> *Astrology, Karma & Transformation* by Stephen Arroyo

Week Three on Progressions

> *The Progressed Horoscope* by Alan Leo
> *The Principles of Astrology* by Charles E.O. Carter
> *Astrology: A Language of Life; Volume I - Progressions* by the present author

Week Four on Lunar Nodes & Life Purpose

The Astrology of Self-Discovery by Tracy Marks

The Astrologer's Astronomical Handbook by Jeff Mayo

Karmic Astrology-Volume I: Moon's Nodes and Reincarnation by Martin Schulman

Week Five on Relationship Analysis Techniques

Skymates by Jodie & Steven Forrest

Planets In Composite by Robert Hand

Karmic Relationships by Martin Schulman

Relationships & Life Cycles by Stephen Arroyo

How To Handle Your Human Relations by Lois Haines Sargent

The Astrology Of Human Relationships by Frances Sakoian & Louis S. Acker

Week Six on Aspects & 360° Cycle Analysis

Planetary Aspects by Tracy Marks

Aspects In Astrology by Sue Tompkins

Dynamics Of Aspect Analysis by Bil Tierney

An Astrological Mandala by Dane Rudhyar

Interpreting The Aspects by Robert Carl Jansky

The Astrological Aspects by Charles E.O. Carter

Astrology, The Divine Science by Marcia Moore & Mark Douglas

Astrology: A Language of Life; Volume II - Sabian Aspect Orbs by the present author

Week Seven on Solar Returns

The Progressed Horoscope by Alan Leo

Interpreting Solar Returns by James A. Eshelman

The Astrologer's Astronomical Handbook by Jeff Mayo

The Solar Return Book of Prediction by Raymond A. Merriman

Astrology: A Language of Life; Volume I - Progressions by the present author

Week Eight on House Rulerships & Dispositors

The Rulership Book by Rex E. Bills

Encyclopedia Of Astrology by Nicholas deVore

The Principles of Astrology by Charles E.O. Carter

Chart Interpretation Handbook by Stephen Arroyo

Saturday Workshops & Tuition Fees

In addition to offering weekday evening beginning and intermediate classes, a professional astrologer can offer Saturday workshops on specific techniques. Because workshops are usually four to six hours long, rather than the two-hour length of an evening class, much more material can be covered.

At my school in Portland, I charged $35 for monthly or twice-monthly Saturday workshops. They were scheduled from 11:00 AM to 4:00 PM, with an hour lunch break between 1:00 and 2:00 PM. These seminars were taken either by students who had completed my beginning and intermediate classes, or by local practicing astrologers who wanted more instruction on a particular technique. Attendance ranged from as few as three to as many as fifteen students per workshop.

As with my classes, I created very detailed handouts for my workshops. Included was a bibliography of germane astrology texts for the subject. My workshops also provided social connections for the students, a place where they could meet others with a common interest in astrology and build relationships and community.

To help with your curriculum development, I will list here some of the topics, along with synopses, that I have taught in my workshops.

Astrology & Anger
4 patterns of anger defined by stressful aspects to Mars, Saturn, Uranus & Pluto.

Neptune in Aquarius (1998-2012)
Previous Neptune in Aquarius periods (1506-1520, 1670-1684, 1834-1848); plus effect on the outer planet generations.

The Ascendant
12 versions of each rising sign; chart ruler; progressed ascendant; transits to the ascendant; Sabian symbols.

Karmic Astrology
Lunar nodes; retrograde planets; twelfth house; interceptions; eclipses; ascendant; the Moon; Saturn; Pluto; transits; progressions.

Jupiter & Saturn
Realms of social and spiritual involvement; by sign, house, aspect, house rulership, transit and progression.

Transforming Loss to Gain
Pluto; Scorpio; 8th house; dark and broken places; loss, death and renewal in life.

The Lunar Nodes
Patterns from past lives; soul purpose; transiting nodes; nodes in synastry and composites; progressions to nodes; planetary rulers.

Electional Astrology
Wedding dates, surgery, starting a business, job interviews; career changes; planetary rulerships; favorable dates and times; what to avoid astrologically.

Multi-Dimensional Levels of Progressions
Secondary, tertiary & minor progressions in their inter-relationship with the natal chart & transits; lunation cycles; retrogradation; stations; 1:13:27 time ratio.

Esoteric Astrology
Spiritual meanings of the planetary glyphs; circle of Spirit, crescent of Soul and cross of Matter; decanates, dwadashâmshas and Sabian symbols.

Sabian Aspect Orbs
Radical new approach to aspects using a 360° model; waxing, waning, applying and separating dynamics; Sabian symbols defining relationships between planets.

Sabian Symbols
History of Zodiac degree analysis; significant natal and progressed degrees.

Medical Astrology
Constitutional analysis; first house planets; 6th-12th house body-mind issues; planetary weakness, Yods; hard natal aspects; progressions; transits; genetics.

How to Cast a Horoscope
Using an ephemeris, tables of houses and an atlas, learn how to erect a horoscope.

Chart Interpretation Skills
Learn how to prioritize the many dynamics found in a natal horoscope.

Chiron
Chiron, discovered in 1977, and its relevance to alternative medicine and holistic healing; transmutation of personal sorrow into loving compassion for others.

Eclipses
Solar & lunar eclipses; frequency & proximity to Nodes; Saros of the Chaldeans.

Family Astrology
Synastry with parents and siblings; composites and multiple composites; ancestral karma found through the IC and its ruler; children's charts; parenting & discipline.

Generational Astrology
Outer planets and collective destiny; Uranus, Neptune and Pluto transits.

Derivative House System
Each house's relationship with the other eleven; rulerships; counting houses.

Minor & Esoteric Aspects
Quintiles, septiles, octiles, noviles, deciles, undeciles & inconjuncts.

Mars, Jupiter & Saturn
Traditional rulerships of Scorpio, Pisces & Aquarius. 2-12-29 year transit cycles.

Spiritual Crisis of Clients
Role of astrologer; virtues and vices of Saturn, Uranus, Neptune & Pluto.

Understanding the Terrorist Attack on America
Pluto in Sagittarius; US Sibly Chart; Saturn-Pluto; prog. US Saturn and Mars Rx.

Jupiter-Saturn Grand Conjunctions
20-year cultural and spiritual paradigm; 800-year Great Cycle; Tecumseh's Curse.

Partners Who Activate Our Shadow
Stressful synastry; attraction-friction; T-squares, Yods; challenging composites.

Selling Your Class & Workshop Tapes

Astrologers can earn extra income from teaching classes and workshops by taping the seminars and offering these tapes for sale locally and by mail-order. You will need to buy an *ultra-miniature tie-clip microphone,* Radio Shack model 33-3013, a cassette recorder capable of high-speed dubbing, and 120-minute cassette tapes.

The lapel microphone sells for $24.99, and comes with a 4 1/2 foot cord. There is a battery unit included with an omnidirectional pick-up, and this little gizmo has an on-off switch that you *must remember to turn off when not in use.* I have only forgotten this once in my teaching career, and it killed the battery; even with doing a sound-check before class started, it did not record properly. Mercury was Rx!

Office Depot no longer stocks the 120-minute blank cassette tapes in retail stores, but they are available by truck delivery. The tapes are a Maxell UR 120 Normal Bias ($3.99 a 4-pack), and these can be ordered by calling toll-free 1.888.GO-DEPOT, item number 332554. There is a $50 minimum for free delivery to your office.

As I wrote in Chapter Two under the section *Office & Postal Supplies,* audio tape labels, Avery #5198 (12 labels/sheet), are also available from Office Depot and are a very professional way to inscribe the class or workshop topic and date.

I made a tape order form for my lecture, class and workshop tapes. I charge $8.95 for lecture tapes, $14.95 for workshop sets of tapes, $69.95 for my beginning class set, and $89.95 for my intermediate class tapes. I include the handouts with each order when I mail these out, and add $1 postage per lecture tape, $2 per workshop, and $5.20 per class set. I use the Postal Service Priority Mail boxes for shipping.

Local Public Speaking & Lecturing

Besides teaching classes and workshops at your school, or at local bookstores, there are an infinite number of opportunities for the self-employed astrologer to earn income through public speaking. I have lectured at Masonic Lodges, middle schools and high schools, Whole Life Expos, local Theosophical Society chapters, metaphysical or spiritual gatherings, salons, and by invitation in private homes.

I have only accepted one invitation in my career to be a *party astrologer,* and it was beneath my dignity. When you are brought in for entertainment purposes, it is noisy, people are drunk, and realistic opportunity for meaningful dialogue is nil.

Now that I am in a different stage in my career as an astrologer, where I receive speaking invitations to lecture and teach throughout the USA, my income is earned from different sources than when I was building my practice. What I valued most about local speaking were the stimulating intellectual relationships I developed with my students. And it helped me develop the confidence in my oratorical skills to evolve into a world-class lecturer.

Chapter Seven

Writing, Publishing & Lecture Travel

Because astrology is such a demanding mental pursuit, and a refined intellect is required for comprehension of this celestial science, many astrologers are highly intelligent people, very well read and make excellent writers. The great joy that I encounter as an author is the intellectual intimacy that I have experienced with book reviewers, editors, my readers and other writers. The Sabian Symbol for my natal Uranus is *The Meeting Of A Literary Society* (23° Cancer).

It is therefore only natural for the self-employed astrologer to branch out into the field of writing for another source of income in his practice. In this chapter, I will discuss getting paid for magazine and journal articles, sun-sign columns, writing for websites, and for submitting research papers. Additionally, I will share my experience of writing books, starting my own publishing company, and earning astrological income on the road through lecturing, selling books and consulting.

I always wanted to be an author. My fifth house Capricorn North Node has been tugging at my soul to do this ever since I can remember. I was derailed for several years by my Cancer South Node in the eleventh house by getting emotionally involved in the politics of local astrology groups and the national organizations.

Because my first book was written at my Saturn opposition at age 44, it came out fully formed, based on the years of practical experience that I had acquired as an astrologer. My vision is to write seven books between that Saturn opposition and my second Saturn return at the age of 59. An additional future goal, after that time, would be to come back to the South Node in the eleventh house and offer service again to the astrological organizations.

Writing is a way to share your consultation experiences, your usage of technique, and your understanding of the conceptual and theoretical dimensions of astrology. There is no substitute for professional experience, but the primary value of good writing in astrology is to help deepen the understanding of others, and to educate them about some of the techniques used within the vast dimensions of this science.

There is also an entertainment quality to good astrological writing, as one who has become conversant with the language of astrology quite enjoys reading a stimulating missive by a fellow astrologer. Humor, wisdom, experience and inspiration are all necessary equal parts of a worthy astrological epistle.

The argument has been made that there are too many astrology books for beginners and not enough written for professional astrologers, advanced students, or the seasoned hobbyist. I completely concur with this, and my goal, both as an author and a publisher, is to yield complex, innovative and creative tomes for this market.

Astrological Journal & Magazine Articles

I have written articles for astrological magazines and journals for the last twelve years, and these pieces were about a wide variety of topics. My subject matter has included *The Uranus-Neptune Conjunction, The Pluto in Leo Generation, Astrology & Twelve Step Recovery, Teaching Astrology, The Effect of Practicing Astrology on Individual Human Consciousness, Secondary Progressions, Sabian Aspect Orbs, The Astrologer as Consultant to the Psychotherapist, The Attack on America* and several other topics, ranging from 2000 to 7000 words each.

These articles have been featured in *The Mountain Astrologer, Considerations, KOSMOS, Geocosmic, NCGR memberletter, The Journal of AstroΔPsychology, The International Astrologer, Réalta* and many other publications. There are additional magazines, like *American Astrology* and *Dell Horoscope*, which have very large subscriber bases, and several different astrological writers contribute to them.

Most magazines and journals have *writer's guidelines* available. They usually request a *query letter*, which is an initial correspondence in which you summarize the content of your intended article. Editors review these queries, and will inform you if they want your article or not. Magazines have a strict policy regarding unsolicited material, so always send the query first.

The payment for articles varies widely. Sometimes, only a trade for advertising is offered, while other magazines will pay writers by the word. A monthly, such as *Dell Horoscope* or *American Astrology*, have Sun sign forecasts, whereas bimonthly magazines like *The Mountain Astrologer* contain forecasts of the generalized daily aspects and the monthly lunations.

ISAR's quarterly journal, *The International Astrologer*, and *NCGR's* bimonthly *memberletter* are examples of organizational publications with articles. There is a highly respected quarterly journal, *Considerations*, which accepts no advertising, is supported by subscriptions only, and is read by most of the top astrologers.

Editors are always looking for well-written pieces, and would be happy to hear of your ideas, especially on hot topics such as current planetary configurations (a Saturn-Pluto opposition or a large stellium in Taurus), or about some newsworthy event such as a president's progressions or an airline crash.

Newspaper & Magazine Sun-Sign Columns

A few fortunate astrologers have syndicated Sun sign columns which are widely circulated in daily newspapers across the country, and are also included on the Internet websites for these papers. In some cases, these columns are *ghost written* by other astrologers. Other gifted writers have lucrative gigs writing Sun sign columns for high-profile glossy magazines such as *Vanity Fair, Cosmogirl* or *Mademoiselle*. There is money to be made with these jobs, but only very few exist.

In your local area, there are weekly magazine inserts that accompany newspapers and focus on food, entertainment or real estate. These newspaper inserts have an editor who may be looking for content. If you notice that there is no syndicated astrology column included, you can phone the newspaper office, speak to an editor and propose to write a Sun sign forecast for the publication.

Sun sign columns are the butt of many derisive jokes amongst astrologers, yet there is a way to write them creatively and intelligently. The best astrological writers use what is known as the *solar house technique.* This is where you place the Sun sign as if it were on the ascendant. Then, you can write about which solar house Mercury, Venus, Mars, Jupiter or Saturn would be in for that week, or that month.

For example, if you were writing the forecast for Scorpios, and that month Mars was in Pisces, by visualizing a horoscope with Scorpio rising, Mars in Pisces would fall in the fifth house. Therefore, for the Scorpio forecast, you could include text about going dancing for fun, or taking the children to the swimming pool.

Similarly, if Jupiter was in Cancer, then, with a horoscope with Scorpio rising, it would fall into the ninth house. For the Scorpio forecast, you could write about going to church with your family, or traveling abroad to visit relatives. This solar house technique is the best method for taking very generalized astrological facts and creatively adding specificity for each of the twelve Sun signs.

Getting Paid to Write for Astrological Websites

Even though I wish it would just go away, the Internet seems to be here to stay. As much as I dislike the illusory world of cyber-community, with so much free information floating around on the web, and no discernment as to value, I admit there are diamonds in the rough here and there, consisting of good writing.

There are a handful of top traffic astrology websites, some already bought out by media corporations, which feature articles, forecasts and columns. Most of the content seems to be geared toward young single women, with Sun sign forecasts, natal and transit reports for sale, love advice, and all very highly commercialized.

Under this tier lies a deluge of countless astrological sites, indistinguishable from one another in their article offerings, columns, and free interpretations of natal horoscopes, which can be calculated right there on the website. Here and there one may find a well-written piece, but, since the assumption of these sites is that people only browse and not read, the article content has been dumbed down to a *USA Today*-like menagerie of superficial sound bites for the ADD web generation.

As you may have surmised, I am quite contemptuous about the Internet, and must be careful not to plunge headlong into Jupiterian pomposity in my disdain for it. My experience writing articles for astrological websites is very limited, and I have only been paid by one. I sent out a trilogy of articles about the terrorist attack on America to the 1450 astrologers around the world in my e-mail address list, and I received many replies requesting permission to reprint the articles online.

One website, *www.Astrologers-0nline.com,* featuring the astrologer Linda Black, was quite professional and offered payment to me for my articles. She sent me a check for $200 in the mail within a few days. Other astrology websites also pay their writers, usually by word count, as with monthly magazines.

The name recognition you gain from your written work for websites will generate secondary income from new clients. There is usually a by-line or bio posted of you at the end of your piece, with an e-mail address given for people to contact. Dozens of individuals wrote me to schedule telephone consults after having had read my articles about the terrorist attack on America.

Research Papers

Another contribution that you can make as an astrological writer is to submit research papers for publication. *ISAR's* journal, *The International Astrologer,* has various research articles printed regularly in its quarterly publication. If you have a quantitative or qualitative research project that you have evolved and refined, you can share your findings with the astrological community in this way.

There are many research topics in astrology still to be investigated and written about. Many astrologers have a pet research project they have kept simmering on the back burner for years, and it would be a shame for this data to remain unpublished. Whether it is research into solar eclipse degrees on local ascendants of airline crashes, or dating habits of women with Venus in Gemini, both types of findings have value and should be shared with other astrologers.

Recently, I received an e-mail from an astrologer in the UK who had seen my writing on synastric progressions in *Volume I.* He informed me that he was doing a study of celebrity relationships in Great Britain, looking for progressed synastry factors on their first meetings, during crisis, and at their break-ups, and would be posting the findings on his website.

This is the type of research project that could more widely expose several hundred astrologers to a technique not commonly used, but quite valuable for analysis of personal relationships as they move through time. I encourage him and others with similar projects to submit their research articles to *The International Astrologer.*

In the book, *How to Start, Maintain and Expand an Astrological Practice*, published by The Organization for Professional Astrology, there is a summary of how counseling astrologers can benefit from research. The author makes the point that, without testing, the plethora of techniques in astrology remain indistinguishable from one another in their relative interpretive value and frequency of accuracy.

Writing Your First Book

At some point in their career, every astrologer thinks about writing a book. Some eventually do, and others never will, and it is a shame that very talented astrologers, with much valuable experience, will leave this earth without writing and sharing that knowledge as part of their legacy.

I, myself, started several books over the years, not getting past a chapter outline for the *next great astrology book.* At the end of 1995, as my secondary progressed Mercury perfected its opposition with my natal Jupiter, my older brother made a very valuable suggestion to me that changed my thinking.

Instead of writing a voluminous 800-pager as I had originally visualized, he made the observation that I might be better off writing a series of smaller volumes, in the vicinity of 150 to 250 pages each. Thus, the *Astrology: A Language of Life* series was conceived. It took me two more years to then get started writing *Progressions.*

In early 1998, after going through a devastating heartbreak in my personal life, I had to rise from the ashes and experience a spiritual resurrection. My progressed Venus had just entered Capricorn, my progressed Ascendant was conjunct natal Saturn, and my progressed Sun was moving into a square with my natal Mars.

Somehow, through the grace of God, the life purpose of my Capricorn North Node kicked in and I learned to alchemically transmute my grief into creative discipline. I wrote *Progressions* that year, started my publishing company, and rebirthed my career after being face down in the dirt with wagon tracks all over me.

Next, I wrote *Sabian Aspect Orbs* during 2000, and learned to incorporate a large research project into a book. While writing the present volume, I have felt the experience of the first two under my belt. If you have the aspiration to write a book, two options emerge: *find a publisher* or *publish it yourself.* I chose the latter.

How to Become a Self-Published Author

When I started researching and writing *Progressions* in 1997-98, I was faced with a big decision. Would I submit my manuscript to an established astrological publishing house, hope for acceptance, work with an editor and a marketing department, and pray that the book would retain its core meaning and value?

Also, being a Scorpio, I did some clandestine investigation into royalty payments, debits from returned inventory by distributors and retail booksellers, and what other author's experiences were working with a publisher. What I heard and discovered was not a pretty picture, financially and otherwise. It took me about three impulsive risk-taking seconds to say to myself, *Go for it!*

I have Mars rising, Jupiter conjunct the MC, nine planets Eastern, and Sun trine Uranus, not to mention a second house Neptune, so I realize that I may be more independent than the average astrologer and more prone to believing that financial visions can come true. For any of us who step into astrological self-employment to pursue our dreams, risk-taking and autonomy are virtues, and I hope that my efforts will inspire other astrologers to also take the plunge.

My publishing company is my retirement plan. I have a vision of writing seven astrology books, and I believe that the cash flow from these book sales, along with the lecturing income that has accompanied my becoming an author, will sustain me in my golden years. After my publishing company stabilizes financially, I plan to create an author's guild, thus allowing me to help publish other astrologers through a shared-expense program.

Starting my publishing company was actually quite easy. To design my first book while I was writing my manuscript, I simply took C.E.O. Carter's *The Principles of Astrology* off my bookshelf, and scrutinized the table of contents, page layout, cover design and title page. Using my 1993 Macintosh PowerBook with Microsoft Works version 3, I created a page template for a 5.5" by 8.5" book, with 0.5" margins left and right, and 0.4" margins top and bottom.

This was accomplished by choosing horizontal orientation in page setup, and the manuscript text would then cover half an 8.5 x 11 page. I had a detailed chapter outline that I wrote from. And to foster a healthy sense of psychological progress as I went along, I would *build the book* page by page, printing each page as I wrote it, folding and cutting the 8.5 x 11 sheet in half with a letter opener to represent the finished 5.5 x 8.5 page.

Little by little, my book became a stack of single-sided laser printed half-sheets on my desk, and holding it in my hands as it grew in size provided a lot of forward momentum for me. I started to think about my book project as if it were a construction job as in my previous career.

There was a scheduled completion date (Jupiter's direct station of 13 November 1998), and all the subcontractors were required by contract to complete their work by that date, or incur steep penalties from the general contractor, such as withheld payment, liens, etc. I pictured myself as the general contractor (publisher), and all of my multiple personalities as the subcontractors (writer, researcher, cover designer, marketing director, etc.).

You will need to include a title page, a table of contents with chapter topics and page number references, and any appendices or planetary tables which will follow the main manuscript. A bibliography can go at the very end, as can your manuscript footnotes. Printing quantities and press run dates can go on the title page. I have also included appendices for my catalogue of lecture, class and workshop tapes, computer chart services, software programs for sale, as well as contact information to encourage lecture, consultation and teaching invitations.

An astrological author must have an editor. No matter how fine a Virgo ascendant you may have, or how exacting a Venus-Saturn conjunction in Scorpio one may possess, there is no substitute for a trained second pair of eyes to go over your manuscript. At this point in my progress, I found a much needed literary associate.

One of my former students, a writer and an editor, agreed to work with me. Patricia Laferriere has made me a better writer by her superb editing of my first two books. I gave her the nickname *Chainsaw* when I first got my edited manuscript back. My long rambling paragraphs were cut into two or three smaller and more concise ones. Patty's stamp on my writing was acknowledged in the following book review of *Progressions*:

> *"Blaschke is an excellent teaching writer. He knows exactly how to introduce his material in small, precisely measured increments, cite his authorities with clarity and brevity, and guide the reader through virtually frustration free assimilation and mastery of progression theory and application. After reading this book and working within the guidelines presented, many of us might begin to wonder why we had not learned these techniques sooner. The answer is that there probably weren't enough teachers or writers of this man's caliber available when we first began the study and practice of astrology."*
>
> *- Joan Star, NCGR Geocosmic Magazine, Winter 2000, pages 98-99*

After moving from Portland to Ashland, I hired an astrologer and fellow writer, Anna Raphael, to be my new editor. Her Virgo Sun went through my manuscript quite meticulously, and she has done an excellent job on this book for me. Her Sun, along with her Taurus Moon, form a synastric mystic rectangle with my planets.

To visualize publishing my book, I made a list of what I would need to acquire and accomplish before my scheduled completion date:

a) an International Standard Book Number (ISBN)
b) a Library of Congress Control Number
c) a scannable bar code for the back cover
d) a retail price

e) cover art

f) back cover photo

g) back cover content synopsis

h) someone to write a foreword for me

i) a software program capable of sophisticated page layouts in order to build a front and back cover plus the book spine into one document

j) quotations from three different printers

k) a financing plan to pay the printer

l) distributors to sell my book to retail booksellers

m) an Advantage Account program with Amazon.com to market my books on the Internet

n) a display ad in *The Mountain Astrologer* magazine to market my books directly to astrologers

o) a data base of book reviewers who write for various astrology publications to send review copies of the book to

International Standard Book Numbers

To create your publishing company, you will need to acquire an *ISBN Log Book* (International Standard Book Number), which is an initial set of ten ISBN's that you assign to each of your titles. These ISBN numbers are the central hub of the existing system for book identification worldwide. They are used to identify the publisher, and for distributors and retailers to place orders and maintain inventory control.

ISBN numbers can be obtained through the United States Agent, *R.R. Bowker Company* in New Providence, New Jersey, by calling toll-free 1.877.310.7333. You will then receive your ISBN Log Book, along with an *Advance Book Information* form that you will fill out and return to R.R. Bowker for your first title. A sample ISBN looks like this: 0-9668978-0-3.

The Canadian Agent for ISBN numbers is the National Library of Canada in Ottawa, Ontario, reachable by telephone at 819.994.6872.

If you do not have a name for your publishing company, you will have to create a business entity for it. In Oregon, this simply means registering the company name with the Secretary of State's Corporation Division Business Registry Office for a small filing fee. Other states will have different procedures.

In California, for example, you have to file your company name with the Office of the County Clerk, and then place a *Fictitious Business Name Statement* in a local newspaper for four issues. I took my existing company name, *Earthwalk School of Astrology*, and used it as the name for my new publishing company.

Once you have established your publishing company, and then add titles as each new book is written, you simply go on-line to *www.bowkerlink.com* and update your title information in their *Books in Print* section. As a publisher, you are responsible for updating this data base as each new title is published.

Library of Congress Control Numbers

Before you publish your book, you must submit a request for a *Preassigned Control Number* [formerly Library of Congress Catalog Card Number]. Forms can be obtained from:

Library of Congress—Cataloging in Publication Division
101 Independence Ave. SE   Washington, DC 20540

This government agency can be reached at 202.707.6372, and has an automated phone system through which you can listen to general information and request these forms. This number is used to classify book content within the nation's library system, *and is not mandatory to have for publishing a title, but recommended.* Once you establish your publishing company, you go to *http://lcweb2.loc.gov/pcn*, join the online program, get an account number and password, and fill out the *Preassigned Control Number* form.

Scannable Bar Codes

No distributor will accept your book into their system unless it has a bar code on the bottom right hand corner of the back cover. This bar code must also contain the ISBN number, along with the cover price and a country code. R.R. Bowker has a list of all *Bar Code Film Master Suppliers* in the United States, and this list can be obtained by calling them at 1.877.310.7333.

Your printer may be able to provide the bar code during the cover-proof phase of your printing job. I got my bar codes from a company in Anaheim, California called *Accugraphix*, reached toll-free at 1.800.UPC.9977. They can e-mail the bar code as an attached EPS or TIFF file directly to you or your printer, and the cost is $29.

Retail Prices

Next, you will have to determine a retail cover price for your book. This is a very important decision with hidden and drastic financial consequences if done carelessly. Book distributor's contractual terms are brutal: they get a 55% discount off of the cover price, then resell your book to the retail bookseller at a 40% discount, thus making a net 15% profit in the process.

They exist on a volume sales basis, and you will not see a dime from them for 90 days after their sale to the retailer, and then you are only paid for the single monthly sales which occurred four months ago. You, as the publisher, will also have to absorb *damage and defective* returns, as well as paying the freight both ways. As you can see, cash flow can be a huge problem for a publishing company.

You have to set your cover price high enough to absorb this discount to the distributor, and you have to print enough copies to get a low enough unit cost per book from the printer. *Volume I - Progressions* has a cover price of $14.95 and *Volume II - Sabian Aspect Orbs* sells for $18.95. I based my pricing decision on three factors: a) page count; b) the printer's quotation for three different press run quantities; and c) my perception of maximum fair retail cost per book.

Cover Art

Deciding on cover art for your book will take you into a creative area of self-publishing. I chose to have an artist paint an oil painting of the Sabian Symbol for my lunar degree, 7° Pisces, as my first book cover. My second book cover is a pastel pencil drawing of the Sabian Symbol for my solar degree, 23° Scorpio.

Volume III's cover is a drawing of the Sabian Symbol for my Ascendant, 22° Virgo. The original works of art are scanned and saved as TIFF files for importation into your cover design software program. My second book also contains several black and white illustrations, done by the same artist who did the cover, and these were also scanned and saved as PICT files and then imported into Microsoft Works as each chapter's frontispiece.

Back Cover Photo & Content Synopsis

You will also need to have a back cover photo taken. I recommend having a friend take this picture rather than a professional photographer. You will save money for one thing, you will be more relaxed and natural, and you won't be persuaded to assume one of those mawkish studio poses with your head cocked to an affected angle and your chin resting foolishly on the palm of your hand. This photo, whether color or black and white, can then be scanned and saved as a TIFF file.

The back cover will require more than your photo, the bar code and the retail price. You will also need to come up with a synopsis of the book's content, your biography as the author, and include excerpts from your foreword. I use bulleted text from my table of contents to serve as my back cover synopsis.

The upper left hand corner of the back cover should contain *Astrology,* and the upper right hand corner should have the retail price. Your publishing company's name and address should appear in the bottom left hand corner, with the bar code placed at the lower right of the back cover.

Forewords

It is customary and traditional to ask another astrological author to read your manuscript and write a *foreword* to your book. Note carefully how this word is spelled. The most common error in self-published books is the misspelling of this word as *forward*. I consider myself very fortunate to have had Robert Hand agree to write the foreword for *Progressions*, Lynda Hill to write the foreword for *Sabian Aspect Orbs*, and Steven Forrest for the present volume.

You can approach an author at a conference, or call them directly and ask if you may send them your manuscript. You should initiate this contact at least four months prior to your desired publication date, as author's schedules are often quite busy and it will take some time for them to get to your project.

Designing Your Book Cover

Now comes the do-it-yourself graphic design phase of becoming a publisher: using your page layout software to design your book cover. I have used QuarkXPress version 3.32 for the Macintosh to create my book covers. First, you need to estimate your final page count and call a printer and have them calculate your book's spine thickness.

For example, *Volume II* was 258 pages, and my printer advised me that the spine would be 9/16" (.5625) thick. Then, go into your software program and create a new document with horizontal orientation. For a 5.5" x 8.5" book, the cover needs to be trimmed to a 8.5" x 11.5625" final size. Make two text boxes of 5.625" x 8.75" size on either side, and put a spine text box of 0.5625" x 8.75" in the center.

The reason that the text boxes must be slightly larger than the trim size is because of *bleed,* w here any element that touches the trimmed edge of the page must be made to extend beyond the edge of the page at least .125" (1/8").

Starting with your front cover, which will be the right text box, make a rectangular picture box in the center which is mathematically proportional to your original artwork, leaving a top margin of about 2", and a bottom margin of about 1.25". Import the TIFF file of your artwork scan into your picture box.

Then, create two text boxes top and bottom. Place your book title in the top box, and your name as author in the lower text box. You can also place the name of your illustrator or foreword writer beneath your name in a smaller font size. Choose a color for the background and a color and style for your font. Make sure you choose *None* for your background color in the two smaller text boxes.

For your back cover, which will be the left text box, you will need to create six smaller text boxes and two picture boxes within it. The two picture boxes will contain your photo and bar code. The text boxes (with *None* selected for your background color) will contain your subject category (Astrology), retail price, foreword excerpts, biography, content synopsis and publisher name and address.

Finally, rotate your spine text box to -90°, and put your last name at the top, the book title or subtitle in the center, and your publishing company's name at the bottom. Congratulations! you have now designed your book cover.

Printer Quotations

Next, you will want to get quotations from at least three different printers to compare prices competitively. You have three options for printing your book. You can offset print both the text and cover, you can offset print the cover and digitally high speed print the text, or you can digitally high speed print both the text and cover. New printing technology, such as the *Xerox DocuTech 6180* machine, can print your book just like a high speed laser printer.

The *Xerox DocuColor 40* machine can digitally print your cover just like a color laser printer. You can supply your printer with *Print Ready Electronic Files* of your manuscript and cover, sent via e-mail as attached EPS (encapsulated PostScript™) files. The only difference in quality between the two printing options is that the digitally printed books will have a slight ripple in the pages, viewed from the edge, similar to a page run through a laser printer with the heat required to dry the toner.

A printing of 500 books will be less expensive using digital high speed printing for both the text and cover. For 1000 books, offset printing will be slightly less expensive. For 1500 books or more, offset printing will be significantly less expensive. To give you an idea of my printing costs, *Progressions,* a 152-page book, cost $6350 for a 2000-copy second printing which was offset printed, about $3.17 per book. Selling this $14.95 book to the distributor at a 55% discount means that I am paid $6.73 per book, a gross profit of $3.56 each.

Sabian Aspect Orbs, a 258-page book, cost $3640 for a 500-copy second printing which was digitally printed, about $7.28 per book. Selling this $18.95 book to the distributor at a 55% discount means that I am paid $8.53 per book, a gross profit of $1.25 each. Now you can see why I don't mind flying around the country lecturing to different local groups, carrying boxes of books with me to sell at the full cover price. It is the only time that my publishing company makes any money!

I recommend the following two printers:

Eugene Print, Inc.   1000 Conger Street   Eugene OR 97402   1.800.688.4741
Thomson-Shore, Inc.   7300 West Joy Road   Dexter MI 48130   734.426.3939

You can shop locally for a quotation from a third printer. I recommend the following specifications for your quotation on a trade paperback book:

> page count (including title pages and appendices) • text = 60# white
> cover = 12 point, C1S (coated one side); 4 color process
> binding = perfect binding in 32's • trim size = 5.5 x 8.5

You can save printing costs by going to a 2-color cover, but you will diminish the aesthetic quality of your book. I realize that with my Mars in Libra, this is an important consideration for me as a publisher. If cost is your primary concern, you could shave several hundred dollars from your printing quotation by doing this.

Financing Plan & Direct Marketing to Astrologers

Unless you have a few thousand dollars in your savings account, or room on your credit card, publishing your first book will require some creative financing. Your printer will have you fill out a credit application, but most likely you will have to pay for the first printing when you go to pick up your books, or before they are shipped to you. I placed an ad in *The Mountain Astrologer*, in the same issue as my book excerpt article, offering a pre-publication discount on *Progressions* to raise money to pay the printer.

This was a smart move for me, as within the first three weeks after the magazine came out, I received over 125 advance orders from eleven different countries, resulting in $2000 of pre-publication book sales. I was able to pay the printer when I picked up my first printing of 500 copies without going into debt, pulling the rest of the invoice amount from the cash flow of my practice and school. Since then, I have been on open account status with them, and have 30 days to pay the invoice after I pick up the books.

Book Distributors

To market your book beyond direct sales to astrologers, you will need to enter into consignment contracts with book distributors. They will order a full case of books from you on consignment (about 35 to 70, depending on how your printer packs them), store them in their warehouse, and ship them to retail booksellers as they receive orders from the bookstores.

The contract terms require you to give the distributor a 55% discount off the cover price, pay the shipping, and you will not be paid until 90 days after the end of the month in which sales were made. The check will sometimes be held an additional 30 days after that. Damaged and defective books will be returned to you, with the book cost and shipping deducted from your payment. There are two major consignment distributors for astrology books in the United States:

BOOKPEOPLE 7900 Edgewater Drive Oakland CA 94621 510.632.4700

New Leaf Distributing 401 Thornton Road Lithia Springs GA 30122 770.948.7845

BOOKPEOPLE ships mostly to bookstores west of the Rockies, and *New Leaf* covers East of the Rockies. You can contact the small press buyer at each company and request a contract be sent to you. They will require a review copy of your book to ensure that it has a bar code, ISBN, proper binding, etc., before they establish your consignment account and send you your first purchase order.

Amazon.com Advantage Account

Amazon.com has an *Advantage* program for small presses and self-published authors. You can establish your account on-line at *www.amazon.com/advantage*. They will also require a 55% discount off the cover price, and you pay the shipping to their warehouse in Lexington, Kentucky. You will have to send them a sample book for a cover scan; they will then build a web page for your book, and also link it by the title and author name in their site search engine.

When I am not lecturing to local astrology groups, this is where I sell most of my books. Customers will write reviews of your book, rank it in a five-star system, and you, as publisher, can have book review excerpts posted on the web page. They pay you 30 days after the end of the month in which sales were made, and you never send an invoice or get mailed a purchase order. Everything is handled through e-mail, except for your check arriving in the mail. I ship my books via USPS Media Mail (book rate).

Amazon.co.uk in England will also carry your book in their on-line catalogue. You can reach them via e-mail at *listing-titles@amazon.co.uk,* and they will send you instructions on how to proceed. However, they do not purchase books through either *BOOKPEOPLE* or *New Leaf,* so you will have to establish another account with either Ingram Book Company in La Vergne, TN (615.793.5000), or Baker & Taylor in Charlotte, NC (1.800.775.1800).

You can call either of these distributors and ask to speak to a small press buyer and they will send you a contract application package in the mail. These two companies are not consignment distributors; they issue actual purchase orders for specific quantities of your titles, and the terms are net 90 days for payment with you paying the freight, as usual. It is worth the extra effort to have your book available overseas, and *Amazon* also has websites in Germany, France and Japan that buy through these distributors.

Book Reviews

When your book is published, you will want to send review copies to astrology book reviewers. My books have been reviewed in *The Mountain Astrologer,*

American Astrology, Dell Horoscope, Geocosmic, AA Journal (UK), AFI Journal (New Zealand), FAA Journal (Australia), NCGR memberletter, The International Astrologer, Considerations, The Wholistic Astrologer (Australia), Aspects, Welcome to Planet Earth, Data News and other publications. Book reviews are far and away the best marketing vehicle for a publisher. One good review in a respected magazine or journal by a well-known reviewer can result in sales of hundreds of books.

One other positive manifestation of being an author is the development of literary relationships with book reviewers around the world. These individuals are highly intelligent, well-read astrologically, and fine astrologers themselves. It is a pure joy to read a review of your book by an individual who fully grasps your theory and technique, and who appreciates the complexities of your writing.

I have only had a single critical book review, with all others uniformly laudatory. I respect the sole reviewer who, while praising the writing, took exception with my core premise for *Volume II.* I commend his integrity for stating his opinion.

Lecture Travel & Earning Astrological Income on the Road

Once you become an author, you have the opportunity to get out on the road and lecture to local astrological associations around the country. On these trips, the self-employed astrologer can earn speaking fees, sell his books, and make money doing personal consultation work.

I have been speaking to local astrology groups since 1989. Prior to my becoming an author, I sometimes received invitations to lecture, based on magazine articles that I wrote for *The Mountain Astrologer.* When my 1992 *Pluto in Leo Generation* article was published in *TMA,* I received invitations to speak to the San Diego Astrological Society and to the NCGR Los Angeles County Chapter in June 1993.

After that speaking trip, I was invited to join the faculty of the *Vision '94* conference, held in Del Mar, California. The following year, San Diego invited me back again to speak, and I also joined the faculty of the *UAC '95* conference in Monterey, California. If you do a good job speaking to local astrology groups, your oratorical skills and professional preparedness will surely be made known to other groups.

Becoming a book author will enhance your professional image and increase the number of invitations you receive for speaking engagements. I have been invited as a guest speaker to the following local astrology groups:

> Oregon Astrological Association
> Eugene Astrology Salon
> NCGR Southern Oregon Chapter
> Washington State Astrological Association

Port Townsend Astrological Guild
Vancouver Society of Astrologers (Canada)
Fraser Valley Astrological Guild (Canada)
San Diego Astrological Society
Southern California Astrological Network
NCGR Los Angeles County Chapter
South Bay Astrological Society
NCGR San Francisco Bay Chapter
NCGR Sacramento Chapter
Arizona Society of Astrologers
Astrological Society of Fort Worth
Astrology Masters, New York City
Philadelphia Astrological Society
Cosmic Circle Astrological Association of South Jersey
Astrological Society of Connecticut
NCGR Boston Chapter
NCGR Berkshire-Fairfield Chapter
NCGR Mid Hudson Chapter
NCGR Cape Cod Chapter
NCGR Richmond Chapter
NCGR Greater Delaware Valley Chapter
NCGR Florida Atlantic Chapter
Astrology Association of St. Petersburg
South Florida Astrological Association
Astrological Research Guild of Orlando

This travel as an author has given me a taste of the astrological community as a whole. I have always been treated with kindness and respect, and I have a lot of love for my fellow astrologers around the USA and Canada. When not staying in hotels, I have been welcomed into the homes of many astrologers throughout the country, and I am very grateful for the warm and loving hospitality given to me. I am equally grateful for the appreciation of my work by these groups.

Usually, I receive an invitation to speak from one particular group in a specific city; then I either *build a tour* by contacting other groups in different cities in that part of the country, or, after other groups hear that I will be in that part of the country, I receive additional speaking invitations from them.

I have had much success in coordinating my speaking tours, and arranging for my travel expenses to be split by the various local groups. I have found that if I communicate with the astrological associations in a spirit of cooperation and love, I receive back nothing but harmonious collaboration. These road trips can sometimes be long and arduous, but I am committed to them as one way to continuously strengthen my publishing company.

While I was national coordinator of the *Professional Astrology Speakers Bureau* for *ISAR,* I designed a standard speaking contract to be used as an agreement between the lecturers and the local groups. My speaking contract calls for a minimum of $150 per lecture, and a minimum of $300 per workshop, or 50% of the gross income, or 67% of the event net income, whichever is the greatest amount. Most of the local groups have been able to pay these fees, and honored the terms.

Airfare expense reimbursement, lodging expenses or housing in the home of a local group member, pick-up and drop-off at the airport, and local transportation of the speaker are included in this contract. Additional clauses call for 10% commission for book sales to be paid to the group, retention of 100% of consultation income by the speaker, and provision of mailing labels by the lecturer from his private data base to the local group for his area clients.

In order to maximize income from these road trips, the astrologer can commit to a busy schedule, lecturing, teaching workshops, selling books, and seeing clients. It is no picnic to go on these trips, especially the one-weekend engagements. I fly in on Friday, speak that evening, teach an all day workshop on Saturday, see clients on Sunday, and then fly home Sunday night. I also contend with the additional travel demands of carrying boxes of books to sell.

To give you an idea of the income that an author can earn from these road trips, I will share the financial details of a trip I took to Texas in April 2001. I was invited to speak to the Astrological Society of Fort Worth. The group was organizing a fundraiser for Kepler College in Seattle, the goal was to raise $1000.

From my selection of lecture and workshop synopses, the group chose a Friday evening lecture on Eclipses, a Saturday workshop on Progressions, and a Sunday workshop on Lunar Nodes and Life Purpose. In addition, they had scheduled a reception and book signing on Sunday evening, and clients for me to see on Sunday and Monday. A local astrologer graciously hosted the reception in her home, and kindly gave me the use of her office for private consultations.

I had modified my speaking contract in order to help them reach their goal for the Kepler College donation. Over that four-day weekend, I grossed $2095. The group paid me $807 ($438 in speaking fees and airfare of $369). I earned $775.00 in consultation income seeing two clients on Sunday morning and four on Monday. I sold $513 worth of my books, 14 of *Volume I* and 16 of *Volume II.*

I am happy to report that the group reached their financial goal for Kepler College. I was able to earn some needed astrological income, and it was a win-win situation all the way around. And I was happy to be treated with the very best of that famous Texas hospitality.

Another example of a lecture trip I took was a longer tour on the East Coast, where I had been invited to speak to four different local astrology groups over a 10-day period. Here, again, are the travel and financial details.

I was invited to speak to the NCGR Berkshire-Fairfield Chapter in Connecticut, the NCGR Richmond Chapter in Virginia, the NCGR Greater Delaware Valley Chapter just outside of Philadelphia, and to Astrology Masters, a private school in New York City. The trip was tightly scheduled, with logistics a big concern.

I flew all day Friday to Long Island from Oregon, then caught a cab to the Port Jefferson ferry to catch the boat to Connecticut. I taught a Saturday workshop there, immediately afterwards I had a seven-hour train ride to Virginia, arriving at one in the morning in Richmond on Amtrak for a Sunday workshop starting at 2:30 PM. Monday, I saw three clients, gave an evening lecture, and then saw four more clients on Tuesday. My hostess had Venus in Cancer, and fed me quite well!

Wednesday, I was back on Amtrak, northbound, stopping in Washington, D.C. to see my brother for a two-hour lunch and a beer. Back on the train to Wilmington, Delaware, where I stayed for two nights, giving a lecture on Thursday evening to the Delaware Valley Chapter, after enjoying a very nice dinner with a group of local astrologers on Wednesday night in the home of my hostess.

Friday found me on the train for New York City. I lectured for Astrology Masters that evening, and taught an all day workshop on Saturday. A delightful group of astrologers took me to dinner in Manhattan after the workshop. I boarded the Long Island Railway in Penn Station going to Islip on Sunday, catching flights to Cincinnati and Portland. I got home, exhausted, from this long trip, having grossed $3697 in ten days. I was paid $1423 in speaking fees and expense reimbursement, I earned $900 in consultation fees, and I sold $1374 worth of my books.

If you are a good speaker, and come professionally prepared with handouts, you will be brought back. The Arizona Society of Astrologers has invited me to speak three years in a row, and other groups on the East Coast, in California, and Vancouver, British Columbia have also invited me back for return engagements.

Chapter Eight

Participating in the Astrological Community

When you begin a professional practice, you are joining the ranks of a loose-knit association of self-employed astrologers who make up a worldwide community. The astrological network is one that you can choose to join or ignore, and there is no obligatory participation whatsoever. I have worked both on the outside and on the inside of this community, and I will share my experience with you.

I had always operated as a lone wolf, on the outside of the greater astrological fellowship, until my secondary progressed Moon entered my natal eleventh house in August of 1990. By the time it had left my 11th house and gone into my 12th in December of 1992, I first moved to Portland, Maine, next to Portland, Oregon, and then became president of the Oregon Astrological Association.

In 1989 and 1990, I had my astrology practice in San Rafael, California, and I spoke in public as part of a monthly group, along with two or three other local astrologers. We would discuss the sign of the month, covering the Sun, Moon and Ascendant. This group was hosted in the home of a colleague of mine, Carlin Diamond, and I joined as a speaker after it had been ongoing for some time.

I moved to Maine in 1990, and while practicing astrology there, heard about a new local group, the Seacoast Astrological Association in Portsmouth, New Hampshire. They met once a month at a hotel along US Hwy 1. I will never forget the first time I walked in that conference room, after driving down the Maine Turnpike from Portland to get there.

Dusty Bunker and Kim Rogers-Gallagher, two astrologers and co-founders of the group, were at the admission table by the front door. I had on a brown suit with a powder blue shirt and a pink silk tie, dressed to wreak havoc amongst the women. Dusty took one look at me and said, *"Scorpio, Virgo rising."* Boom! Nailed on the spot! I thought, *"this astrologer knows her stuff."* It was right then that I felt an inner urge to be part of this group, to learn to appreciate the knowledge of others.

The former speaker of the U.S. House of Representatives, Tip O'Neill, once said that *all politics are local.* This is quite true within the astrological community. The core strength in our profession lies within the local astrological associations in the various cities and towns around the world. These groups support individuals and their practices, and promote community education.

In this chapter, I will discuss participation in local astrology groups and national organizations. Professional astrology has both its lone wolves and its community members. As Uranus enters Pisces in 2003, in mutual reception with Neptune in Aquarius, our profession is at the threshold of potential spiritual solidarity. I have some thoughts on what can be done to help make this happen.

Service & Membership in Local Astrological Associations

As a self-employed astrologer, you will be forming new relationships with clients, students and customers. For the economic survival and growth of your practice, you will have to love and serve these people, recognizing their value to you as the source of your income. The bottom line is that you really do not have to answer to anyone else as an astrologer other than to these patrons.

You may wish to remain isolated from the other astrologers in your community. However, I recommend forming relationships with colleagues and practitioners who may become friends. A central environment for these alliances to take root is in your local astrological association.

Local groups are made up of regular people, who are the salt-of-the-earth within the greater astrological family. There, in this cross-section of astrological humanity, you will find hobbyists, amateurs, beginning or intermediate students, part-time professionals, full-time expert astrologers, and the top authors in the field. The common denominator is simply a shared love of astrology.

One way to understand how this network of relationships operates is to contemplate the eleventh house, which rules groups, colleagues and associates. The trine to the third house shows how students will be attracted into your school of astrology from the group. The trine to the seventh house illustrates the clients that you will gain from participating in local groups.

The sextile to the first house represents the self-confidence you will develop by being seen as a professional by your peers. The sextile to the ninth house portrays the education obtainable through mingling with other astrologers and hearing of their spiritual insights and their understanding of astrology.

There are also self-regulating mechanisms within local astrology groups, designed to keep a community in a healthy balance. The opposition to the fifth house depicts how any arrogant and Napoleonic behaviors by an individual within the society will be met with resistance. I am guilty of this tyranny myself, as transit Pluto was forming five conjunctions to my natal Sun when I *rose to power* in 1992-3. My heavy-handed methods to reform the local group made me some bitter enemies.

The square to the eighth house describes how public money and income, i.e. dues collected by the association, must be spent according to the will of the majority, or result in a conflict between the board of directors and the membership. The square to the second house characterizes how any astrologer who uses the group strictly as a source of revenue for their private practice will be challenged by members.

All of these relational dynamics, mentioned above, serve to teach the individual astrologer that he is part of a greater good. Social conduct and personal and professional integrity are foundations of a healthy community. Many astrologers have given service to their local associations, and, as a result, have strengthened their careers. Keeping the balance is key.

Most local groups are non-profit entities with a board of directors, and a few at-large positions such as taping of speakers, maintaining the group's library, media liaison, etc. The groups usually meet once a month for a Thursday or Friday evening lecture, and a Saturday workshop on that same weekend. The board may meet once a month as well, to discuss organizational business.

My biggest complaint about the local astrology groups are financial. In 1991, I felt that the Oregon Astrological Association, which has proven to be typical of other groups around the country, was not charging enough for lecture and workshop admission, thus not earning sufficient speaking fees for the visiting lecturers.

On top of this, the board of directors sometimes swelled to a dozen or more people, none of whom were paying for lectures and workshops, and who sometimes made up one half to one third of the total attendance at meetings. I perceived this as a freeloading culture of dead wood for an organization, and was determined to perform surgery and eradicate it from the association's body.

As you can imagine, with transiting Pluto conjunct my Sun back then, I was using a howitzer to kill a grasshopper. I proceeded to start a riot within the group, which I had only just joined the year before. That fifth-eleventh house opposition certainly kicked in big time, and many members stopped coming. My first response to this was *good riddance, who needs these parasites anyway?*, but, over the years I have come to see the error of my ways and I now feel remorseful.

As you might deduce, Scorpios, or at least this one, with Sun square Pluto, are not wired for group process (natural square to Aquarius). For me, with reform-minded Uranus in my eleventh house of groups, I decided to retire from community politics and focus on writing my books, making my contribution to astrology in another way. However, before doing just that, I had some successes bringing well-known astrologers and authors to Portland, and earning them substantial speaking fees, book sales and consultation income.

I had visualized a business model of success for the local group, which consisted of four venues per season (September through June) when we would bring in a national author; and for the other six meetings we would feature local or regional astrologers as speakers. I felt that the membership would only be willing to pay higher admission for lectures and workshops four times per year.

I invited Tracy Marks, a well-known and respected author from Boston, to lecture and teach a workshop in Portland in 1993. We offered a pre-registration discount and publicized her appearance to the membership. I then included a flyer for her presentation inside my newsletter, which was mailed to 2000 people on my private mailing list. Immediately I was accused of a conflict of interest, and much resistance was stirred up by the locals over the admission prices, and the fact that I combined marketing of the event with Earthwalk Astrology.

Now, I have come to realize that native Portlanders can be somewhat provincial, but, back then, I didn't understand this. I was trying to get them to see themselves as world-class, requiring top-notch astrology. Frankly, it was like selling a Ferrari to a bumpkin, and all they could think of was *how much hay can it tow?* Over the years, I came to love these people, and I believe that they love me, too. But I tried to push change too fast for their liking.

Transit Pluto was crossing over the organization's Midheaven at that time, and unquestionably, things had to transform into a new shape. It was an ugly job - but somebody had to do it - and Mr. Scorpio took on the calling. We could only get three people to accept nominations for service on the board of directors, with the rest of the rabble choosing to let the association wither and die on the vine. I ran the OAA for a year with only a secretary and a treasurer.

The irony is that, after all these years, the group is still going stronger than ever, and is using the business model for speakers and events that I re-introduced in 1992. My lesson from this is that reformers and transformers can create change, but may not make many friends in the process. To the OAA's credit, when it was first birthed in the 1970's as the Portland Astrology Association, high quality astrologers such as Diana Stone and Donald Weston designed a similar program.

By telling these stories, I am trying to illustrate the realities of local astrological politics, which can be just as brutal as any other segment of society. Getting people to agree with one another, especially astrologers, can be almost an impossible task. Love is the only method that I know of to help resolve the differences of opinion, requiring very refined leadership abilities. As a younger man, I did not have these virtues.

If you feel called to give service to your local astrology group, it is a noble effort. The groups only remain in existence because of the work and dedication of individuals. I found a direct cause and effect relationship between participation in local groups and the growth of my career.

In Appendix I, you will find a comprehensive listing of local astrology groups in the USA and Canada. Contact them to inquire about how to join and serve.

Service & Membership in National Astrological Organizations

Inherent in the profession of astrology is a structure of organizational leadership, regulatory oversight and education. In the U.S. there are four major astrological organizations, first mentioned in Chapter One under *Organizational Certification* and *Mentorship & Apprenticeship*. These four national societies are:

1) The American Federation of Astrologers *(AFA)*
2) The Association for Astrological Networking *(AFAN)*
3) The National Council for Geocosmic Research *(NCGR)*
4) The International Society for Astrological Research *(ISAR)*

Each group has an area of focus benefitting individual astrologers. *NCGR* has local chapters and an esteemed system of education, testing and certification. *ISAR* provides a forum for research papers, professional development and ethics training. *AFAN* maintains a focus of media watch, legal support and community networking. The *AFA* has long been a bastion of local group affiliates, teaching, book publishing and offering correspondence courses in astrology.

How does an astrologer, serving at the local level in his hometown group, get involved with these national organizations? If you do something noteworthy, you will be approached by them. There are eyes and ears out there in the astrological community's grapevine, and a good job will be recognized, just as a major *faux pas* will also get some press. It is not that astrologers are gossipmongers, only that an organic network has evolved through the decades to insure the overall well-being of the profession.

Demographically, the astrological community is presently split into generations. The Pluto in Cancer assemblage, making up a majority of the *AFA* membership, consists of souls born between 1912 and 1937-9, and many of these astrologers are now concentrated in retirement environs such as Arizona and Florida. The Pluto in Leo flock, predominantly baby boomers born between the early 1940's and mid-1950's, are the largest segment of the astrological population, and occupy most of the current positions of leadership in *AFAN, ISAR* and *NCGR*.

A growing concern is a demographic drop-off within the Pluto in Virgo generation (1957-1971), in which there are substantially fewer numbers of astrologers. What remains to be seen is whether there will be a resurgence of desire to practice astrology amongst the Pluto in Libra beings, born between 1971 and 1983-4. The oldest have just had a Saturn return, and the youngest are now reaching college age. The future of astrology rests on the shoulders of this group, and it is my hope that this book will be an incentive for them to see astrology as a viable career.

In 1993, I wrote an article about my experiences with the Oregon Astrological

Association and submitted it to the *ISAR* quarterly journal, *KOSMOS*. I detailed how I had put together our program for the year, specifically, the bringing in of Tracy Marks, the late Jim Lewis and others to speak. Admission prices, how much we paid the lecturers, book sales, expense reimbursement, consultation income and earnings for the group treasury were included.

I didn't hear anything back from the journal editor for over a year. Then, around Christmas of 1994, I got a call saying that they wanted to publish the article. The next Spring I joined the faculty of the *UAC '95* conference in Monterey, California. A President's Council meeting was held, attended by the heads of the local groups from around the country. At this meeting, I was asked by the then *ISAR* president, Ray Merriman, to become National Coordinator of a new *Professional Astrology Speakers Bureau*. I accepted the position, and joined the *ISAR* board.

My story illustrates how service in your local astrological association can lead to contribution in the national organizations. What I then did for the *Speakers Bureau* was to create a data base of every local astrology group in North America and put together a portfolio of 20-25 lecturers, with the intention that the Bureau would arrange speaking trips for the authors and lecturing astrologers.

Ray and I also designed a standard speaking contract to be used as a negotiating platform between the lecturers and the local groups. This agreement specified that a speaker would receive a minimum of $125 per lecture (now $150), a minimum of $250 per workshop (now $300), or 50% of the gross income, or 67% of the event net income, whichever was the greatest amount.

Likewise, airfare reimbursement, lodging expenses, housing in the home of a local group member, pick-up and drop-off at the airport, and local transportation of the speaker were included. Clauses for a 10% commission for book sales, retention of 100% of consultation income, and the providing of mailing labels by the speaker to the group for area clients were also in the contract. This agreement has become the *industry standard,* and most local groups honor its terms.

When this new program was launched later in 1995, it all looked great on paper, and *ISAR* had high hopes for its success. However, in practice, the *Bureau* encountered some major logistical problems with the various astrology groups.

For example, a particular group would invite a lecturer to speak and teach a workshop. Then, I would contact other groups in nearby cities to inquire about a second and third stop for the speaker on his trip. I found that the groups had fixed meeting nights, such as the first Thursday or the third Friday, and there was not always enough flexibility for a multi-stop speaking trip to be scheduled smoothly.

There were some successful trips arranged, but, in the end, the work I had done did not result in a completely fortuitous undertaking. What *ISAR* chose to do was to make the local group data base public domain, and have the portfolio of lecturers available to any group who requested it. Bottom line, each astrologer had to set up their own tours.

During this involvement with the *ISAR* board from 1995-96, I learned what goes into running a major astrological organization. Board chemistry is crucial, as is skilled leadership by the president; and devotion to astrology as a profession is essential to be able to put in long hours of volunteer work, as I did.

The perceived negatives that I encountered were typical backroom politics that exist in any organization, like who gets speaking slots at conferences and other perks for service to the establishment. Although I loved my fellow board members, and very much enjoyed working with them, I made a personal decision to resign from astrological politics and write my seven books. This way, if I received invitations to speak, it would be based strictly on my work, and not on who I knew or what connections I had. I have never regretted this decision.

If you have a desire to serve at the national level, I have a tip for you. Do a good job for your local group, and national service will find you right where you are. The cream always rises to the top, and you do not have to schmooze, brown nose or name-drop to get somewhere within the profession of astrology. Let your hard work, and the quality of who you are be your calling card.

Referrals & Professional Courtesy to Colleagues

Another way to participate in the astrological community is to treat your fellow astrologers with love and respect. In practice, this means to graciously refer clients that you do not have the expertise to help, or cannot fit into your schedule, to one of your peers. I have a Portland colleague, Mark Dodich, who exemplifies this ideal. Each time I have referred a client to him when my schedule was overloaded, or because I have moved, he has sent me a referral check of $15.

One of the worst belief systems that an astrologer can fall into is *scarcity fears*. If you are struggling financially with your practice, it is only human to begin circling the wagons and become fearful of competitors who might detract from your business. Nothing could be further from the truth. A rising tide lifts all boats, and the self-employed astrologer will find that the more he spreads the business around, the more will return to his practice. Referrals to your colleagues will help preserve your income.

It creates such sadness for me to see how astrologers sometimes treat one another. Envy, backbiting, gossip, rivalry and cronyism are the evils of our vocation. One goal to hold in your heart is for the profession of astrology to improve its standing in the world by ameliorating the relationships and conduct between astrologers. Our greatest enemy is not rejection by the academic establishment or by *CSICOP* and *The Skeptical Inquirer,* but the infighting that exists within our own ranks.

It is my opinion that, when Uranus ingresses into Pisces in 2003-4, the profession of astrology may reach levels of solidarity not seen since the 1920's. The young Charles E.O. Carter, at that time assuming the presidency of the Astrological Lodge of the Theosophical Society in London (upon the death of Alan Leo), led our profession to a level of impeccable dignity through the gentlemanly qualities, combined with the deep spiritual wisdom found in his work.

The legacy left behind by C.E.O. Carter, incontrovertibly the finest astrologer of the 20th century, was his brilliant intelligence and the honorable regard for his colleagues which graced his work. If there were to be a role model for the young self-employed astrologer to emulate, it would be Carter. He was the best, and much of present-day astrology's interpretive knowledge has evolved from his labors.

From his pen, during the last sojourn of Uranus through Pisces, flowed some of the most exalted books in astrological literature. *An Encyclopædia of Psychological Astrology, The Principles of Astrology, The Zodiac and the Soul, Symbolic Directions in Modern Astrology, The Astrology of Accidents, Some Principles of Horoscopic Delineation, Essays on the Foundations of Astrology, The Astrological Aspects* and *An Introduction to Political Astrology* are all remarkable testimonies to the Sun trine Uranus genius of this great astrologer (born 31 January 1887).

Salons, Internet E-Mail Groups & Message Boards

In recent years, a peculiar form of participation in the astrological community has emerged with the advent of the Internet. In 1995, as Uranus ingressed into Aquarius and Pluto entered Sagittarius, international astrological mailing lists and newsgroups came out around the world. Using group e-mail, these lists provided astrologers a greater access to each other, as well as opportunity to circulate their dialogue.

An advantage of this form of community is the ability for isolated astrologers who live in remote and rural areas, with no proximity to local group meetings, to find discourse with other practitioners of the celestial science. A bizarre network of astrology subcultures has evolved out of the initial amorphous cyber soup. By 1998, when Neptune ingressed into Aquarius, an entire online society of digital inhabitants could be found, representing every conceivable branch of astrology.

An absurd downside of this phenomenon, which we can baptize as *Holy E-Grail,* is that a real, live astrologer might be living down the block from you, with whom you may never speak, while you are writing to a faceless soul in Finland or Japan.

It has been my observation that the Internet, and modern technology in general, has contributed to the deteriorization of civility in western culture. Astrologers, who may be somewhat lacking in social dexterity to begin with, seem to have gone off the deep end with the World Wide Web, blindly believing in the high tech gods of modems and cyberspace. It is my hope that some of us will choose a return to pre-Internet communication methods, such as telephone conversations and letters.

Here in Ashland, my friend and colleague, Mary Plumb, and I began a monthly astrology salon as a response to the September 11th terrorist attack on America. We perceived a great need in the local community for conversation about world events, and wanted to offer an analysis of the massive geopolitical realignment resulting from the Saturn-Pluto oppositions, which fall on the USA chart horizon.

Mary and I have been holding these salons in the living room of her home, with a fire burning in the fireplace, tea and talk afterwards, and a sense of real warmth with those in attendance. I can only speculate that those trying to make a buck on the Internet have, because of its inherent illusion of true community, attempted to attribute human qualities to a technological medium devoid of heart and soul.

One can pray, with Uranus ingressing into Pisces, and squaring the natal Uranus in Gemini found in the horoscopes of those responsible for this Internet madness, that they will have a deep spiritual awakening, see the error of their ways, and dismantle their websites in favor of *real* human relationships.

Perhaps astrologers will tire of the Internet and all of its cellophane non-substance, and once again return to actual human connection and real astrological discourse with one another in person. It is my hope that the events of 11 September 2001 will transform the reality of society and draw us all closer to each other.

Astrologers *can* use the Internet positively to reach out to colleagues. One medium for this is *Message Boards,* such as those found at *The Mountain Astrologer* magazine's website. Here, there are topic *strings,* which are chronological listings of initial postings with their subsequent responses.

Message boards are maintained by an individual who periodically cleans up the inflammatory rhetoric, deletes months-old digital postings, and answers questions left by visitors to the website. Some individuals will only be looking for free astrological guidance, and within the *Laws of Cyber Co-Dependency,* there are equal numbers of advice-givers for every lost soul looking for a free, quick fix.

These interchanges can demean professional astrology, as they expose the younger generations to the central evil of the Internet, *free information with little real value.* The great challenge of modern astrology, in my opinion, is to reverse this alarming trend, chastise the robber barons of the Web trying to make a fast buck, and return to the previous distribution system of knowledge and consulting within astrology.

Professional Ethics, Collusion & Other Considerations

As could be expected, with Pluto transiting through Sagittarius from 1995 to 2008, ethics, morality and principles have come to the fore as top priorities. Within the professional astrological community this has certainly been the case, as some of the national organizations, such as *ISAR* and *NCGR,* have attempted to create ethics training seminars for practicing astrologers.

Predictably, much dissent has resulted, primarily because *ISAR* used a therapist model of professional conduct to structure its recommendations. Many astrologers view themselves as independent consultants, not psychotherapists. Therefore, trying to fit the glove of therapist conduct onto the hand of a typical self-employed astrologer would be missing a thumb and a pinkie. Recalling the OJ trial, *if it don't fit, you should acquit.*

I feel that what *ISAR* is trying to accomplish *is* necessary for astrology at this time in history, but that they are going about it in the wrong way. A different, and I believe, better, approach has been proposed by Arlan Wise of *The Organization for Professional Astrology.* She suggests professional astrologers form local peer-review groups, where client problems, counseling techniques, improper behavior by a colleague, and other matters would be discussed.

The intelligent logic behind this approach being superior for ethical improvement amongst astrologers lies in its local and personal format. Any attempt to mandate moral ascension for the typical self-employed astrologer on the national level is going to miss the boat. True and lasting change can only be created and maintained on the local level, supported by the development of real personal relationships.

In the corporate world, one of the most grievous sins to commit is collusion. This occurs when price-fixing, obfuscation of defective merchandise, or other actions are undertaken to deliberately deceive and connive customers. Not a pleasant subject to discuss, but it exists within the astrological community, just as it does in every professional environment.

Collusion takes place when astrologers, in positions of organizational power, use their business connections in order to achieve personal financial gain. To pull off a *fait accompli* such as this, there must be a silencing of other astrologers who might otherwise be compelled to whistleblow thieves into shame and repentance.

I have obliquely observed this happening within our community for years, and I have found it to be disturbingly justified as *business as usual.* It is against the law in the outside world, and it should be against the law within our vocation as well. Fear of reprisal by those in power serves as the cover for these nefarious activities to continue year after year.

If you observe activity such as this going on, I would hope that your conscience would compel you to speak out about it. Outcries from astrologers about attacks from the academic establishment, critique from scientists, or condemnation from the religious community are hypocritical if we do not clean up our own act first.

I have often wondered if astrologers could ever have *a true community.* I have never accepted Uranus as the ruler of Aquarius, but assign Saturn to the Water Bearer. The romantic and self-centered vibration of Uranus, commonly known to rule the profession of astrology, is diametrically opposed to the often humane qualities of group relationship that fall under the domain of Aquarian sociability.

The enduring memories that I have of experiencing astrological community are all quite Saturnian. An elderly local group president who has served with honor for many years, the self-discipline and dignity of a mature astrologer advising a younger colleague, the recognition that experience is the most valuable asset an astrologer can possess; all positive sides of Saturn in true astrological community.

I want to end with praise for all of the local groups and national organizations who bring astrologers together to find greater strength in fellowship, camaraderie and brotherhood. Despite our humanity and failings, a spiritual responsibility to protect the profession through group solidarity will always exist.

Chapter Nine

Overcoming Occupational Hazards

Without a doubt, there are many consequences involved with entering into self-employment and launching a practice of astrology. When you own a business, the work is never done, and the self-employed astrologer will have to learn how to adjust to this reality. This voyage will demand that you develop time-management skills, self-discipline, and a balance between other aspects of your life and work, as well as learn to cope with the world's reaction to the profession of astrology.

Many of the experiences of the self-employed astrologer are common to anyone with a private practice, or to any small business owner. We must deal with financial uncertainty, living without benefits and the security of employment. Perseverance, patience and a resolve to succeed must be developed. However, there are specific peculiarities and occupational hazards attached to the practice of astrology, and I will discuss these factors with you in this chapter.

Most astrologers start out with high ideals about their professional services, and how they want to help others using astrology as a healing art or a counseling tool. Soon after beginning the practice of astrology, however, financial pressures set in. The need to learn business and marketing skills become equally as important as a mission statement and spiritual intentions.

The practice of astrology will change you and make you into a highly resourceful person. If you do not quit, and you are determined to see it through to completion, building a successful astrology practice is a life-long lesson in faith, belief in self, and in embracing a creative way of life. What is also true is that not everyone is cut out for, nor has the temperament for, self-employment. I have watched several astrologers give up and go back to their day job, and, for them, it was the right thing to do.

It is my belief that self-employment requires a few basic astrological dynamics to be present in the natal horoscope in order for that person to make it. Among these are Uranus aspects to the Sun, Ascendant, MC, or the chart ruler. Risk-taking and living on the edge are quite Uranian, and the practice of astrology is under this rulership as well. To a lesser extent, the same aspects from Mars can also help.

Planets in fixed signs and in succedent houses are essential for self-employment, as determination is necessary to meet hurdles and challenges head-on. Jupiter or Neptune in the second or eleventh houses, or aspecting their rulers, is also helpful for being able to impetuously follow a financial vision and believe it to be obtainable. Entrepreneurs are often born at the first quarter Sun-Moon phase.

Some Taurus, Virgo, Scorpio or Capricorn is priceless when you own a business, as hard work, organizational skills and financial acumen are a must for success.

The Self-Employed Experience Jupiter Cycle

Realistically, it will take you twelve full years to build a successful practice. This is the Jupiter cycle, ruling financial prospects and the professional life. It takes many years for a referral network to mature and for repeat clientele to become an established part of your business. It is better for you to have a sober resolve to keep at it for at least a dozen years, than to have a *laissez faire* approach, thinking that natural laws will build you a practice full of clients. There are few free lunches on this earth.

I started my full-time astrological self-employment in July of 1989, when I reached my third Jupiter return at the age of 35. I moved to Portland, Oregon when transit Jupiter sextiled my natal Jupiter in August 1991, and it was there that I built my successful astrology practice into what it is today. At the waxing square of my Jupiter cycle in September 1992, I began to teach a regular class schedule, along with Saturday workshops, as part of a major commitment to build my school.

In October 1993, at the waxing trine in my Jupiter cycle, I had my best month yet for clientele income, and my national mail-order report business was in full swing. At my Jupiter opposition in December 1995, I left Portland to move to Seattle to be near my elder daughter. I had major business expenses to market my practice and school in a new city. I kept a second office in Portland, and would commute there to see my clients. I sure learned about over-extension the hard way.

At the waning trine in January 1998, I had to draw deeply on my inner wisdom and accept the painful fact that a personal relationship which brought a second child into my life was not going to make it, and I would have to accept defeat and start over again, to rebuild my career as an astrologer. By the third of the three waning squares of my Jupiter cycle, in January 1999, I had written *Progressions* and started my publishing company.

At the waning sextile in May 1999, the very positive book reviews for *Volume I* started pouring in, and I was invited to lecture in several different states. At the waning semisquare in April 2000, entering the balsamic phase, I had launched the huge research project for *Sabian Aspect Orbs*, and began to write *Volume II*.

When I reached my fourth Jupiter return in June 2001 at age 47, I knew that my astrology practice and publishing company had been built on solid rock, and that I was now free to leave Portland for a better quality of life. Shortly thereafter I was invited to join the faculty of the *ONLINE College of Astrology*, which enabled me to move to Ashland in September 2001 and begin writing this present volume.

My experience in building my business over these twelve years is a prototype of what any self-employed astrologer might expect along the road to success.

Financial Stress & Worry

The primary occupational hazard to overcome as an astrologer is financial stress, and worrying about uncertain income. There is no easy way to conquer this, as it is your *baptism of fire.* The question of how badly you want the freedom and independence of self-employment will be a constant challenge for years, and getting there will extract a painful pound of flesh from you. Being a full-time astrologer is akin to taking the vows of priesthood, where one must embrace poverty, obedience and even lunacy.

I am here to tell you that *it can be done.* Not easily, but it won't kill you, either. My Virgo work ethic is ingrained in my soul, and, with four planets in Scorpio, *I do not quit.* I have been broke, and I have wrung my hands in desperation on the last day of many months, when my office and apartment rents, car insurance and credit card bills were all due. Somehow, though the years, everything has been paid for.

I never missed a month of child support payments, and I never starved to death. My second house Venus, Saturn and Neptune have all contributed to my financial and spiritual initiations. Neptune gave me the belief and the vision that it was possible to make it as a full-time astrologer. Saturn has taught me endurance and what honor and character are all about. And Venus gives me the love for my astrology business, which was the only force that I could find to overcome the fears.

Self- mployed astrologers need to help each other. We must provide emotional and spiritual support for our brothers and sisters in practice by encouraging them to hang in there when times are tough. I once dated a Cancer woman who used to wait tables, and I was always moved by how generously she tipped other waitresses when we went out to eat together. There was a love and a solidarity that she felt for them, and she expressed it with a plentiful tip.

As I wrote in Chapter Three on cash flow, you will have weeks where you earn $165, and another when you make $2300. There will never be a routine income that you can count on week-to-week, so, in time, you will adapt and learn to look at your income from a monthly, quarterly and yearly vantage point. Even long-time professional astrologers, in practice for 30 years or more, still have the experience of fluctuating clientele income.

My personal solution, and my recommendation to you, is to view days with no clients as writing days, mail-order days, or teaching days. Everything that you do as an astrologer, be it consulting, writing, teaching, shipping out books, tapes or reports, is all part of an overall effort that builds your income on solid ground.

There is a spiritual place in your heart that you can go into, in order to cope with financial stress and worry. It is your faith and belief in yourself. *The Lord helps those who help themselves.* It is only your fear that can bring you down and make you quit. And it is only your love that can conquer this.

Academic, Scientific & Religious Community Condemnations

Once you become a professional astrologer, you will inevitably experience some criticism, scorn, ostracism and condemnation from the academic, scientific and religious communities. I have my Sun trine Uranus, and I always greet these personal impertinences with a *screw you* attitude. I must admit that my middle finger has been cocked like a pistol trigger for many years now, but, with age, I have slowly begun to moderate my defiant demeanor.

For the thin-skinned astrologers amongst us, these occupational hazards can be a bit unnerving. As I wrote in Chapter Six, my beginning astrology class at Portland Community College was abruptly cancelled after the college president received a letter from a Christian fundamentalist decrying the curriculum as *pseudo-scientific.* This goon, in one fell swoop, managed to pull a coup in all three categories: I got hit with a left jab by the religious right, with a right cross by the academic Puritans, and knocked on the canvas by scientific ostracism.

I also a remember a dinner party in Arch Cape, Oregon. I introduced myself as a *professional astrologer* to a husband and wife who came up to meet me, and he said, *"that's not a profession."* Three options flashed in front of me in a nanosecond; should I punch him, riddle his mind full of bullet holes with my superior intellect, or swallow my pride and do a Jesus by turning the other cheek? I chose the latter.

I once dated a woman who was a medical doctor, an anesthesiologist at my local hospital. We had a composite Sun square Jupiter, and she would make references to astrology as *my amusing belief system.* Well, within a week of her Chiron return at age 50, she was fired from her job at the hospital in a political power struggle with the department head, and wouldn't you know it, she then began to ask me about that *spiritual transformation* and *Chiron return thing.*

The most painful memory I have of condemnation of my astrology practice came in the most personal area of my life. I entered into a relationship with a woman who was an old friend of twenty years, and whose grown children I was Godfather to. She had become a born-again Christian, after being a disciple on the same Eastern spiritual path as me for ten years, and we had a child.

Saturn was transiting through my natal seventh house, and everyone in her life opposed me. Her church, her pastor, her family, her small town community, and her grown children all objected to the relationship. I can vividly recall the pastor's wife sitting on a sofa in the living room, telling me how God would not want astrology in the life of my infant daughter. After I explained how the baby Jesus was saved by Chaldean astrologers (Magi), she waxed into an attack on *the occult*. '

It occurred to me right then and there that narrow-mindedness and ignorance are the most sad qualities of the human condition, and that no logic would penetrate the mind of an irrational zealot. So, once again, this old warrior had to surrender to defeat, and lose the woman and child that he loved dearly in order to continue on with his profession of astrology. I have paid my pound of flesh, I assure you.

The goodness and love in astrology is measured by the benefit it provides for your client. There is no victory in debate with scientists, academics or religious fundamentalists. Astrologers actually weaken the profession as a whole when we strike back blindly at our critics. Our strength as a profession lies in the love and support that we can provide to our clients, and to one another.

Isolation, Alienation & Loneliness

Whether you work from home or lease office space, another occupational hazard of practicing astrology is isolation, and the feelings of alienation and loneliness that go along with it. This problem is also common for those with any private practice, or for individuals who are independent consultants.

There is a social function attached to being an employee of a business, and seeing one's co-workers each day at the office, plant, store or warehouse. The astrologer, on the other hand, while seeing clients, or speaking with them over the telephone, does not have *sustained and consistent daily social relationships*. This, in my view, is the root cause of the isolation that plagues so many astrologers.

What can the self-employed astrologer do about this? The problem is greatly exacerbated if the astrologer is single, divorced or widowed, and does not have an emotional support system. Many single astrologers suffer doubly, and when combined with ostracism from the scientific, academic and religious groups, a very real sense of alienation and loneliness intensifies the isolation.

Therefore, friendships, community, dating and making effort to develop personal relationships, along with regular contact with one's children, siblings, family and other relatives, becomes crucial for sustaining the astrologer's emotional and spiritual health and well-being. I, myself, have serious doubts about the medicinal benefits of the Internet and the so called *cyber-community*. Yet many astrologers seem to get enjoyment out of communicating by e-mail with their online buddies.

Alienation is ruled by Uranus, and isolation or loneliness are Saturn-ruled, so it occurs to me that Chiron, which orbits between these two planets, is the key to the solution for the self-employed astrologer. If one recognizes that they have feelings of alienation and loneliness, then my recommendation would be to reach out and offer friendship, companionship and love to fellow astrologers in your hometown.

Patience, Faith & Perseverance

The virtues of patience, faith and perseverance are essential for the self-employed astrologer to remain in practice through the years, and overcome any occupational hazards that challenge his will to continue. Patience is a Saturnian virtue, and to develop it, the astrologer must learn to think with a long-term perspective. Despite any hurdles in your present circumstances, always maintain a seven-year plan and a fifteen-year goal. Then, any current setbacks will seem much smaller.

My personal method of doing this was to establish my publishing company, with a plan of writing seven astrology books over a 15-year period, between my Saturn opposition at age 44 and my second Saturn return at age 59. When I feel down about some upset in my daily, weekly or monthly experiences, I lift my chin up and remember the mountain peak I have chosen to climb.

Faith is a Jupiterian virtue, and comes quite naturally to those astrologers with a preponderance in the fire element. Those of us lacking such fortification will have to develop this asset through devotion to our clients (water emphasis), social and intellectual purpose (air emphasis), or through pragmatism and ambition (earth emphasis). Faith is the spiritual requirement for believing in your eventual success.

If you have the Sun, Mars or Jupiter on an angle, especially the Ascendant or the Midheaven, but are lacking in fire, life will feel like a public show of enthusiasm while you are privately miserable and consumed with worry and self-doubt. Of this, I know much about, for, with Jupiter on my MC, and no planets in fire, I am seen professionally one way, while my intimates know of my hand-wringing.

Perseverance is both a solar and a fixed-sign virtue. I have been beaten up pretty thoroughly in my personal life, as you may imagine an astrologer with Venus in detriment conjunct Saturn would be. Each time, after being sprawled out in the dirt, my ever-romantic Pisces Moon looks up and muses, *"that wasn't so bad."* Without my Scorpionic determination to fulfill my life purpose as an astrologer, I would have given up long ago. Fixed signs are extremely determined, and like the *Timex* watch ads of yesteryear, *"we take a licking and keep on ticking."*

The Impact on Your Personal Life

There are occupational hazards associated with the practice of astrology that may directly impact your personal life. I was a self-employed astrologer for a few years while married. I long to return to this state one day, when I can find the right Mrs. Earthwalk, but the majority of my years in practice have been as a single person. I have been on the receiving end of various rejections.

I really do not know if my personal experiences as an astrologer reflect the norm, or if these life episodes are more to do with my Sun square a 12th house Pluto, and my Venus-Saturn conjunction. Either way, they have served to substantially humble me, and contribute to the development of compassion within my heart.

I was once told by a woman, *"You self-employed guys are all alike. You do $90,000 worth of work each year, and you only have $20,000 to show for it."* Ouch! That exchange left me feeling inferior and poor, yet inside, I was thinking, *"f... you."* Astrologers may not feel as secure or prosperous as an employed person, and besides, we wouldn't want to be in a relationship with another who would evaluate our worth by how financially useful we were to them.

One of my venial sins as an astrologer, which has negative impact on my personal life, is when I calculate the horoscope of a woman I have recently met and have an interest in, and then form assumptions in my mind about who she is before I have the chance to just get to know her. This is done by most single astrologers, of course, and it will require some self-restraint to avoid doing this. It is justifiable after a few dates, when you are considering the potential of deeper involvement, but, in my experience, be avoided during the first month after meeting a new friend.

Another toll taken on my personal life by being an astrologer is my tendency to astro-analyze everything that is going on, with a resultant loss of feeling, grace, intuition and instinct about my life circumstances. This is observable at astrology conferences, where overheard conversations contain snippets such as *"his Uranus squared my Moon, and I was so attracted to him, but we argued all the time"* or *"man, she was gorgeous, but that Saturn of hers on my Mars was the worst!"*

Human interaction will occur as it should, regardless of whether or not the astrologer looks at the synastry and composite charts of those with whom he has personal relationships. It may be an advantage to resist curiosity, and go *astrologically blind,* at least initially, into possible relationships.

As I wrote earlier in this chapter, astrologers will sometimes be rejected by others with strong religious beliefs, academic or scientific prejudices against astrology, or irrational fears about the occult or paranormal phenomena. When this happens in your personal life, as it has to me with my younger daughter, the wound can be quite deep, and perhaps only another astrologer could understand what the experience of alienation and rejection may have felt like. This is another reason why self-employed astrologers need one another for mutual support.

Living With No Medical Insurance or Retirement Plan

When people ask me who my HMO is, I can only reply with a single word, *"God."* I have not had medical insurance for 13 years, simply because I could not afford it.

I have been to a county medical clinic once, and sat in the waiting room with all of the immigrants who spoke no English. I also went to an acupuncturist once; other than that, I have been healthy, and believed in the regenerative powers of Scorpio.

I realize that my experience is not for everyone, especially parents who have children living with them, but I also feel that there are certain things in life that you can do without. I have been asked, *'What are you going to do if your appendix bursts?'* Well, I just don't think about that kind of stuff. Health care and worry, in my mind, are two sides of the same coin.

You might ask me, *"Robert, did you arrive at this philosophy out of necessity?"* The answer is yes. In building my astrology business, I just did not have enough money for everything that I had in the previous chapter of my life when I was employed. Some things had to go. Medical insurance was one of them. I didn't have the best teeth, either, when I began astrological self-employment, and now they're worse.

This is a reality that astrologers have to deal with. Even with high deductibles, a medical insurance monthly premium can be over $300. If you have office rent, home mortgage or rent, car payment and insurance, groceries, utilities, etc. to pay, where is this extra money going to come from? I may be foolish, and sitting on a time bomb ticking away, but, so far, it has been one more thing that I could do without in life.

I hoped for alternative medicine health care insurance to materialize when Chiron transited through Scorpio. That did not happen, and the Clinton disaster in trying to establish universal medical coverage made it feel even more out of reach. I am 48 years old, and perhaps I can hang in there until Medicare kicks in later in life.

A self-employed astrologer has no retirement plan, either. This, and health insurance, used to provide security and peace of mind for workers. With the recent Enron debacle, and the losses suffered by the fallen giant's employees, more of the population is realizing that we are on our own financially. I have felt like this for 13 years. Economic insecurity can be a particular challenge for single astrologers.

Insurance is ruled by the eighth house, and retirement by the twelfth, both being of the water element. It would then stand to reason that control and fear underpin a perceived need for this protection in life. My personal approach has been to view my career as an astrologer as a calling, therefore making effort to strengthen my faith in believing that I will be cared for and guarded by spiritual preservation.

There is a saying, *"praise God, but tie the reins of your horse."* Even though I might sound like one of those religious fanatics who never take their children to doctors, I'm not, and I have tried to plan ahead for my retirement by establishing my publishing company. I don't have any other sensible advice to give you here about living without medical insurance or a retirement plan. I wish us all good health.

Consultation Burn-Out

Many individuals in the helping professions, such as nurses, therapists, healers and other types of caregivers, may find themselves approaching burnout from the various stresses associated with their work. This can be an occupational hazard for astrologers, as well. Whether due to the overscheduling of appointments with clients, absorption of too much vibrational energy during sessions, or competing demands from other areas of life, astrologers may sometimes need a sabbatical.

There is no shame in this. Astrologers are human, and, like anyone else, may need an occasional time-out. Warning signs of burn-out can be: feelings of resentment for having to listen to client problems, feelings of indifference toward voice-mail messages left by clients, feelings of dread when clients schedule appointments, and loss of concentration when looking at charts while preparing for a client.

Certain progressions or transits are notorious for producing these symptoms. A hard Neptune transit to your natal Venus or seventh house ruler will blur the boundaries with clients. Progressed aspects from Mercury to Uranus, or transit Uranus to Mercury, can fracture your attention and make concentration difficult. Saturn on the Ascendant, conjunct, square or opposite your natal Sun, or itself, can feel like you are staggering under the oppressive weight of too much work.

I have taken a sabbatical twice in my career as an astrologer. The first time was when I had a broken heart and I was unable to work for two months. The other time, I planned in advance to bail out of my practice and write *Volume II* while Neptune was stationing, and square to my natal Venus for six months from July 2000 to January 2001. I went broke, drank a lot of wine, and floated in astral trance states, encircled by Sabian Symbols and the sacred geometry of Zodiac harmonics. There are chapters in that book I do not remember writing.

If you find yourself struggling with your clients, please take the initiative to call a fellow astrologer and talk about these things. It can only get worse when kept in the shadowy realm of subconscious denial. You will feel 100% better by simply stating these feelings out loud to another. Local peer review groups can help here.

Teaching Burn-Out

Another form of burn-out may plague teaching astrologers. Since most classes are taught in the evening, and the self-employed astrologer may already have worked during regular business hours seeing clients, it can make for a very long day. Even with my Virgo rising, and all my tenacious Scorpio, when I had my school I would sometimes be so exhausted by ten at night that I could hardly think. I taught two or three nights a week for years, in addition to my full-time practice and mail-order business, and I vividly recall utter mental fatigue.

I finally realized that two nights a week was my limit for teaching. I sometimes felt my passion waning, so I had to cut back my schedule to rest and revitalize. There are usually a few teaching astrologers in every city. Refer students to a colleague's classes when you need to take a break. There will be no loss in business for you, as the referrals will be reciprocated.

Sustaining Your Practice Through Personal Loss & Tragedy

Like other human beings, astrologers will inevitably experience loss and tragedy at some point during their lives. These episodes may result in much spiritual growth, wherein the astrologer, through his own ruin and grief, can then feel more love and compassion for his clients than before. I have personally traveled this road of sorrow and spiritual resurrection, and it has made me a better astrologer.

When I was young, I relied on impeccable technique, consummate preparation, intelligence and good communication skills to connect with clients. But, my heart was not fully open. I can remember sitting in my chair during consultations, with a tight feeling in my solar plexus and throat chakra. With all of my water planets, I am very empathic. But, to be honest with you, my channels were not fully open.

I have written elsewhere in this book about my personal losses in recent years, and how I rose from the ashes. Many astrologers go through troubled times, and it is their work that can keep them going through the pain. For those of us with Scorpio planets, eighth house planets, or hard aspects to Mars and Pluto, loss can be a great teacher. How does an astrologer sustain his practice through a tragedy?

My recommendation is to develop vulnerability with your clients, freely admitting loss and failure. The astrologer becomes more human, and is less likely to be perceived by the client as only a detached spiritual authority. I used to only observe my client's lives. Now I feel deeply what they are going through. I am much closer to my clients now.

Your astrology practice can be sustained through any hard years by your wisdom, and through your commitment to put the needs of others above your own concerns. Jupiter is the planet of preservation in life, and, as such, its virtues are required to go through personal loss while maintaining the ability to serve others. We all feel universal emotions and sympathies that can be shared with others. It may be that consciousness is not fully realized until it is washed in the blood of the heart.

The Mythological Experiences of the Career Astrologer

The last occupational hazard for the practicing astrologer that I will discuss with you involves the ascent or descent into the archetypal realms. Seamless is the fabric that unites astrology with mythology, as it involves ancient stories of supernatural beings that serve to explain aspects of the natural world, and to delineate humankind, society and culture.

When using the language of astrology the astrologer merges with these Zodiacal and planetary forces and is thus taken into a borderline realm of consciousness where reality and symbolism converge. It can certainly feel like a journey into the abyss when the astrologer discovers that his own life has begun to resemble the landscape of the classical domains.

Most people experience life in a frame of reference originating with their parents, education, religious training, and acculturation. This adaptive philosophy will change throughout the life of an individual because of the necessity for memory to order itself with retrospection and reminiscence. However, an astrologer, through his work, is aligning himself with the entire and unbroken chain of human history.

Thus, to use a scientific metaphor, brain functions within the minds of astrologers are operative at root, or core, levels of cognitive reasoning. Because of this, the perceptual reality of the career astrologer evolves over the years into a level of depth quite alien to the average human being. The result of this places astrologers in the position of experiencing their life at archetypal and mythological levels.

For the Neptunians amongst us, this is just grand, and welcomed like their wedding day. Uranians, too, will also delight in this experience, as their minds and nervous systems are composed of astral and causal elementals. The ascent of consciousness into these realms is a far cry from the sorrowful descent of pathos into Pluto's underworld kingdom, or the futility of attempting to pass through Saturn's rings.

To give you a personal example, I was born with Ceres rising in Virgo, and my story of losing a daughter is quite mythological. My mother was born in 1922, and has natal Saturn square Pluto, as does the mother of my daughter, born in 1956. My mother's chart ruler, Saturn, is at 7° Libra 46', and my daughter's mother has her ruler, Mercury, at 7° Libra 43' Rx. This is the midpoint of my natal Mars and Black Moon, and was triggered by my progressed Last Quarter Moon in 1996.

Since I have gone through this heart-rending tale of loss, many clients have come to me with an angular Ceres, or with her conjunct one of the Lights. In each and every case, there was a lost child; by adoption, abortion, stillbirth, suicide, runaway, infant death, or Child Protective Services because of substance abuse or alcohol.

Was it my archetypal experience that gave me the compassion to work with their loss and grief? This I will never understand, but it is my belief that a mythological resonance exists between astrologers and clients.

Chapter Ten

Fostering Personal & Spiritual Growth

In this chapter, I want to discuss with you how the self-employed astrologer can grow, both personally and spiritually, through his work. I also want to look at some of the ways an astrologer can cultivate and nurture themselves in order to avoid burn-out, excessive eccentricity, and the feelings of alienation. Sometimes, when I have neglected to do this, I felt like a wizard living on the fringe of society.

These issues, many solved with simple common sense, apply to any self-employed individual. One must learn what is required to maintain balance between work and the other areas of life. Yet, again, there are peculiarities about spiritual growth that are specific to the practice of astrology, and I will share my failings and victories with you regarding this personal struggle.

I have clear past-life memories of being a medicine man, shaman, healer, medieval alchemist and physician-astrologer. The longer I have been in practice, and away from the corporate world, the more distinct these memories have become for me. Anyone with retrograde planetary rulers of the angles (Mercury and Jupiter for me) is off of the linear time-line to a great extent, and goes back and forth between this life and previous incarnations. I want to be honest with you about my experience.

It has become increasingly obvious to me that the urge to become an astrologer did not originate for me during this lifetime. I came out of the womb with Uranus conjunct my South Node, and in an exact trine with my Sun. Hello! I was born to be a professional astrologer, and was blessed with a prototypical horoscope for this work. Is this innate urge to practice astrology part of a greater calling for additional spiritual growth in this lifetime? I think, yes.

Astrology, as a profession, is a precious rarity in that it allows the individuals who practice it to remain continually connected to the Divine kingdoms, the Spirit planes, and to the archetypal and mythological realms of consciousness. To be able to earn a living while existing in this celestial environment is, in my mind, a phenomenal blessing and opportunity for spiritual development.

When I was a young man, I always felt torn between my role in the world and my inner, spiritual self. I perceived that I had my 'work' and my 'real work.' The urge to make these two into one never let up, and was a relentless force driving me to become a full-time astrologer. Was this force my soul purpose communicating to me that I needed to become an astrologer? Yes, it is my calling, and I followed it.

James Hillman, in his book, *The Soul's Code* (Random House; 1996), articulated an 'Acorn Theory,' wherein the unfolding of the *daimon,* or the genius inherent within the soul, is supported by all life experience, be it childhood trauma, adolescent turbulence, or the adult evolution of consciousness. This spiritual imprint was in place as the soul incarnated, and serves to prompt the personality throughout life.

Professional astrology is a calling, and much more than a simple career choice. Therefore, if the call is heeded (which, for me, and for many other astrologers, occurred at the entry of the secondary progressed Moon into the Crescent phase), the astrologer needs to be aware that there are spiritual consequences that will reverberate at a soul level, and which require deep, personal integration of subconscious forces.

These forces, in my view, are karmic in nature. That is to say, they accompany the soul between lives, and re-emerge during the present incarnation. The Sabian Symbol for the degree of your progressed Moon, as she waxed Crescent 45° ahead of the secondary progressed Sun, is highly informative and illustrates the specific nature of how the astrologer answers the calling to practice.

My Crescent phase commenced on 21 August 1978, in the 3rd degree of Aquarius. The Sabian Symbol for this degree is: *A deserter from the Navy stands suddenly committed to a dawning truth; freedom is never the result of compromise* (Lecture Lessons by Marc Jones; 1931). At that time, I took an astrology class with William Lonsdale in Vermont, and resolved, on an inner level, to become an astrologer.

I was just 24 at the time, and had been studying astrology since 1971, but up until then, the urge and calling had only partially been realized. I hitchhiked across the USA and Canada quite a bit during the 1970's, at times carrying an ephemeris and tables of houses with me in my backpack, and I would do charts in exchange for food, a roof over my head, long rides to the opposite coast, or some good pipeweed.

My lottery number for the selective service was higher than those who would be drafted in 1972 and therefore I did not serve in the military during the Vietnam War. I understand this Sabian Symbol and its desertion theme to mean that I was called to live a life *outside the box* in terms of work and spirituality. By following this call, I found my freedom. It also helps to explain my uncompromising attitude about being a full-time astrologer, rather than keeping a day job and only practicing part time. I have never regretted this choice, no matter the obstacles.

I have a very distinct memory from 1976, intensely etched into my soul, when I read *Karmic Astrology, Volume I,* by Martin Schulman, about a Capricorn North Node: *"Through the North Node an image is established which others can look up to and model their lives after. At times personal difficulties deplete him of the strength to hold up this image, and yet hold it up he must, even if it means sacrificing his entire life."* I cannot tell you how many times, while staggering through my sorrow and failure, I drew strength from reading this passage, resolving again and again to one day reach the top of the mountain so that others would have a trail.

Walking the Talk

One of the more difficult experiences I have had as an astrologer is when I felt like a hypocrite, dispensing celestial and spiritual guidance to my clients, while not living up to these standards in my private life. I would guess that any astrologer might have felt this way at one time or another.

I have two things to say regarding this. Firstly, I needed to develop compassion for myself, and realize that it takes many years to mature as an astrologer and as a person; and it can take time to bounce back from a painful loss or failure. Clients and students will never hold you to any standard of perfection in your personal behavior; it is only within your own mind that these self-critical voices operate.

Secondly, I came to see that the astrological language represents an ideal, and that none of us can ever measure up to these intentions all of the time. The astrological cycles and their succeeding spirals help to explain this. One may strive sincerely toward an aspiration (for example, during a Jupiter return), and perhaps be only partially successful in obtaining the goal. At the subsequent Jupiter return, the individual may find that he is now drawing nearer, and will continue onward.

What does *walking the talk* mean? In a nutshell: *don't ever advise a client to do something that you yourself cannot do.* The fact is, an astrologer sets himself up for feelings of hypocrisy by communicating with clients from a place one step removed from his own truth. *If you are in your truth, you will always speak that truth.*

I have had some utter disasters in my personal life which left me reeling, holding onto the lamp post, and wondering if I could just make it through the day. What do you do when a client is scheduled to appear that afternoon at your office, and you feel like you are death warmed over? I don't know what other astrologers have done, but there were many days when I concluded a consultation, then promptly went downstairs to the back porch of my office building to drink a beer and smoke a cigarette. I can remember feeling so split while doing this.

Then it dawned on me that the truth of my life during that time was that it hurt. I began to stop communicating from a position of astrological detachment with my clients, and, instead, tried to become more modest and vulnerable. Immediately, I felt a huge burden lift from my shoulders, and I was free to just be me, and not have to represent some spiritual ideal of consciousness as an astrologer.

This realization has been important in allowing me to enjoy my work. No longer do I have to think of myself as some sort of spiritual expert on all matters, human and divine. What a relief! What was I thinking? For me, perhaps that big ol' Jupiter on my Midheaven originally swelled this younger man's head, but after several women showing up in my life with puncturable hat pins of extreme karmic sharpness, I assure you that I have been well-seasoned on the barbecue spit of life, and I am now more soulful and humbled.

To walk the talk as an astrologer will require some emotional support from your colleagues. I encourage all of my readers to start a peer review group in your hometown and invite other astrologers into a safe environment where personal challenges can be freely discussed.

Meditation, Prayer & Personal Renewal

Make no mistake about it, practicing astrology full-time will require some daily inner maintenance and spiritual renewal. Some astrologers, especially those with water signs rising, Neptune aspecting the Ascendant, or a watery Moon, will be vulnerable to absorbing vibrational energies from the client, and will need to learn techniques of cleansing and regeneration to preserve their health.

In alchemy, the poison contains the cure. This is like taking the venom from a snake to produce an antidote for bites. Each of the four elements contains this dichotomy. The fiery astrologer will provide much inspiration for his client, but will need physical exercise each day to avoid impatience. The earthy astrologer will give much practical advice to his client, but will have to stick to a strict personal routine in order to provide consistently sound and reliable guidance.

The airy astrologer will produce much intellectual understanding for his client, but without daily social involvement in his own life, will lose perspective and objectivity. The watery astrologer will offer much spiritual insight to his client, but must remain devoted to his work, and emotionally nurtured in his own life, in order to maintain compassion.

How can the self-employed astrologer renew himself on a daily basis? I believe that astrologers need to pray, meditate or reflect so as to remain integrated, and to nourish intuitive faculties. The demands of life, such as the needs of children or spouses (not necessarily in that order!), can interfere with the necessity for the solitude that is so essential for appointment preparation.

I experience my work as an astrologer as sacred, and I pray for spiritual guidance and protection to help my clients with their problems and concerns. There is a marriage of technique and intuition that occurs when angelic help is requested for interpreting horoscopes. The astrologer may find that he does not want to stray too far from this place of spiritual connection.

For astrologers to be present and spiritually grounded during consultations requires personal insight and effort to remain in your own center of gravity. Those of us with retrograde chart rulers will have an easier time of this, as our natural state is to be more oriented toward internal streams of thought or feeling.

Exercise & Nutrition

Two very basic, yet essential, requirements for self-employed astrologers to stay healthy and to do quality work are regular exercise and excellent nutrition. Exercise is ruled by Mars, and explains how physical movement affects brain functions. Nutrition is ruled by the Moon, and by the sixth house, and therefore influences empathy, responsiveness, and attitudes of service toward your clients.

My happiest daily routine as an astrologer is walking everywhere that I need to go. I have had the good fortune of living and working in cities or towns where I could create this kind of lifestyle. Presently, in Ashland, I work from a home office, and I walk five miles every day into downtown and back. I enjoy this very much and look forward to it daily, as it clears my head, keeps my legs and lungs in good shape, and gets me out of the cottage to avoid that cooped-up feeling.

I go to the post office to pick up my mail, I stop at the bank to make deposits, and I walk down Main Street past all the shops and cafes. Some days, I will stop at the grocery store on the way home. I usually schedule my two telephone clients at 11 AM and 3:30 PM. This allows me to get my walk in during daylight hours in the winter, have lunch, and still leave time to prepare for the afternoon client.

For years, I had my office in downtown Lake Oswego. I was also able to walk to the post office and bank, and I got to know every postal clerk and teller by name. When I was writing *Progressions,* I would take these one-hour walks through a State Park and back, going straight uphill to the Nature Center, breathing hard, and then hauling it downhill back to my office. I would especially love this walk at dusk, when the nature spirits were out, and their astral bodies were twinkling.

I was miserable when I had my office in Southeast Portland on Hawthorne Blvd., as the neighborhood looked like an infernal scene from Genesis 19. I saw enough body piercing, ropeheads, tattoos and counterculture riffraff to last me for the next forty years. I was a pony-tailed bohemian myself during the 1970's, but I guess the younger generation has to go to further extremes to shock their ex-hippie, baby-boomer parents. Plus, the post office was too far away to walk to everyday.

In the morning, I do 150 sit-ups, 40 push-ups, and two sets of 10 chin-ups. This gets me going first thing, and then I have my English Breakfast tea (with two sugars and cream, of course!) and answer my e-mails. With my Moon in the sixth house, I feel a lot of comfort in sticking to my routine. I had to overcome mild addiction at times with that Moon in Pisces and, fortunately, it only got as bad as 4 smokes a day. I am happy to report that I have quit for some time now, and feel in great shape.

Not being much of a cook, I am no nutrition expert. I have been a vegetarian since 1975, and have found this diet, which I originally took to for spiritual reasons, is quite conducive to mental deliberation. Astrologers certainly need to have good concentration when preparing for consultations, as well as during sessions, and I find a lacto-ovo vegetarian diet (includes dairy and eggs) works well for me.

I have to eat three meals a day, or else my blood sugar drops. I find that I do my best astrological preparation work, as well as writing, about an hour after meals. These exercise and nutritional considerations may sound pretty basic to you, but, believe me, if you get out of your routine, the quality of your work may drop. When I am on the road during lecture travel, I find I need to bring food with me on the plane, or in the car, so as not to feel irritable when I am eating irregularly.

Partners, Friends & Family

For a self-employed astrologer to grow spiritually, as a person and through his work, it will require an emotional support system. As I wrote previously about occupational hazards associated with practicing astrology—isolation, alienation and loneliness—these can creep up on you, and affect the quality of your work by depleting your emotional body of its strength.

The role of partners, friends and family in the life of an astrologer will be very important. My experience has shown me that relationships with clients, although limited to the preparation time prior to the appointment, and to the consultation session itself, require a lot of energy from the astrologer, and thus limit the amount of activity the astrologer can share with the important people in his personal life.

These time demands on the astrologer, requiring seclusion for preparation prior to consulting, can be difficult for other family members, especially spouses and children. In this situation, the astrologer may be better off having an office outside of the home. As you can see, the balance between a need for privacy to do the astrological work, and the need for nourishing human relationships, may conflict. I have found that it is possible to regulate this through limiting my schedule.

For years, I scheduled clients everyday of the week, except Sundays. Some days, I would only have one client, but it turned out that the work day would center around the appointment, and my time management efficiency suffered. I also found that I was constantly thinking about my work, and never had any down time, even when I was with people outside of my practice.

It wasn't until I started writing my books that this way of scheduling changed, and only then because it had to. Now, I schedule clients one week, then the next week I write, alternating week-to-week. This schedule serves to keep me time-efficient. During client weeks, I schedule eight or ten clients in four to five days, rather than dinking and putzing around with one client per day. The week that I am writing also frees me mentally to relax more, as I don't feel pressured by the next appointment. I thus have more time to be social with friends, as well.

I have friends here in Ashland who are very near and dear to me. If you are a single or divorced astrologer, these friends are worth gold, and can be your sole source of emotional connection. One other very important relationship for me is with my older brother, whom I talk to regularly over the telephone, especially when I have to make business decisions about my publishing company. He is invaluable to me for the practical advice, enduring love and emotional support he provides his younger brother living on the edge.

With Mars in Libra, I am so much happier when I have a girlfriend, and my work is much more filled with joy when I have companionship to look forward to. But, as you may imagine, with a Venus-Saturn conjunction, I have also had chapters in life where I had to go it alone, and was not blessed with love and romance. I have always tried to give equal quality astrological service to my clients, whether or not I had love in my personal life. This has been an ongoing challenge for years.

I also very much appreciate my relationship with my older daughter, who is 21. She has been around astrology from day one (Dad manually cast and hand drew the chart for her birth in 1980), and I get a lot of enjoyment out of looking at the synastry for her and a new boyfriend. Her roommates have also received regular e-mailed analyses of their composite chart dynamics with boyfriends, I might add.

Although client relationships are intimate and meaningful, personal relationships in your life, outside of the context of astrological service, are essential for a balanced and nourishing emotional life.

Hobbies Outside of Astrology

I am not the guy to write this section of the book, but without a co-author, you're stuck with me. As you might presume, with my obsessed and relentless four planets in Scorpio, a workaholic Virgo rising, and a Mercury trine Uranus that is only interested in what interests me, I am not the most well-rounded person. It feels good to admit this to you, kind of like being on *Oprah* during disclosure week. However, I am blithe to report that I am now working on this balance in my life.

I will never know if it really required the single-minded and ruthless devotion over the last thirteen years to get me where I am, or if I could have had more fun along the way. I almost don't want to know, so I won't have to feel that I missed something (like a life). Now, at age 48, and in the first year of my new Jupiter cycle, I feel the need to make improvements in my life that will help foster more personal and spiritual growth.

I took piano lessons as a young boy, and I can vividly remember Madame Hodell whacking my knuckles because I didn't have my hand bridged properly. I also recall the gold stars I got on my sheet music for performing *Tarantella* from memory during a recital. I would very much like to play the piano again, and perhaps even compose music. Maybe the Venus-Saturn conjunction favors this later in life, yes?

I also enjoy travel, and the social side of my lecture trips as an author. I have met many astrologers in the local groups around the country on my trips, and, with Cancer on my eleventh house cusp, these people are like my extended family. I have happy memories of conversations with other astrologers in their homes, as I was graciously hosted by them while speaking in their city. One in particular stands out, in a dining room on the waterfront in Miami, overlooking Biscayne Bay.

For those of you just starting out with your astrological practice, perhaps you can learn from my foolishness and make a concerted effort to balance your astrology work with your personal and human needs. Hobbies, family and friends will help keep you well-rounded, and will serve to regenerate your love for astrology.

Going Through the Inevitable Hard Times

Despite my lunar Piscean idealism, I am a tough Scorpio warrior who has taken a pounding, and kept on going forward against all odds. I am also a pragmatic Virgo who understands that work usually has to come first in order for a business to succeed. One of the creative conflicts I have encountered in writing this book, was whether to be forthcoming about the struggle, and therefore show the reality of self-employment as an astrologer, risking that my reader may be scared off.

The other option would have been to sanitize and glamorize the experience, thus possibly attracting more young people into the profession, but leaving them unaware of the mandatory tests of character, endurance and stamina necessary for full-time astrological self-employment. If you have gotten this far, and didn't do a retrograde Mercury by reading from back to front, you can see that I have taken the former approach, choosing to be honest and realistic with you.

Astrology, as a profession, is still not fully accepted by the mainstream, and may never be. Your mettle will constantly be tested. Being an astrologer will sometimes feel like you are living on the edge of society, without full recognition. Thus, astrological self-employment is not for everyone, and, as I wrote in the previous chapter, requires basic horoscope dynamics such as Mars or Uranus aspects to the Sun or MC, along with fixed-sign planets for the requisite determination.

If you are not frightened off by my stories and experiences, then you will have what I have—the peace in your soul that you are not a quitter, and that you show your love for astrology by sticking with it through thick and thin. There will be the inevitable hard times—being broke and right on the edge financially, or classic comebacks from heartaches—but, if you persevere, you *will* grow spiritually.

Chapter Eleven

Notes for Astrologers in the UK & Australia

It was my hope to make this volume relevant for all self-employed astrologers, not only in North America, but also abroad. Toward that end, I asked two colleagues from overseas to contribute to this chapter. I am indebted to Paul F. Newman of the UK, and to Scott Whitters of Australia, for writing these summaries about the practice of astrology in their countries.

Astrology in the UK by Paul F. Newman

Although the Witchcraft Act was only repealed in Britain in 1989, as far as I am aware it has never actually been illegal to make one's living as an astrologer in the UK. Unusual maybe, but it is not illegal. However the Witchcraft Act, which comprised a set of laws originally laid down by Parliament in centuries past, was always woolly in regard to astrology. And to this day there is no rigid code, no special licence that is required by law before you can set up in business simply as an astrologer. Neither, as it stands at the time of this writing, is it mandatory to have an academic qualification in astrology before deciding to make this one's profession. (It goes without saying that if you were intending to open up a booth to read horoscopes on a street corner you would have to obtain the appropriate licence from the Local Authority. Or if you were applying to teach astrology officially at an Adult Education venue you would most likely need to show some form of qualification of your abilities.)

As for any form of self-employment, you would need to inform the Inland Revenue (Income Tax Office) of the date on which you began your new business, and in due course fill in an annual Tax Return giving a statement of your profit or loss. If you are going it alone as a 'sole trader' there is little else you need to do officially, other than to keep a record of all your income and expenditure transactions. It is not legally necessary to employ the services of an accountant on your behalf, although if business is booming and paperwork not your forte, a good accountant can undoubtedly save you money. If you intend to set up a business that employs other people there will obviously be more legal considerations, but whatever your use of astrology might be (for example: opening a specialist bookshop, giving face-to-face consultations, writing Sun-sign columns from home...), it does not differ from any other form of business just because it is 'astrology'.

However astrology is different (from, say, being a conventional bookshop owner or a teacher) because it is easy to feel isolated and cut off from one's colleagues in the same profession. Luckily there are many organisations, schools and societies within the astrological landscape of the UK that can be of great help in providing both moral and practical assistance. (See below for further details). The importance of one to one or small group supervision as a support for one's practice should not be underestimated, nor the chance to exchange views with others by attending a local astrology group. Although they are independent of each other and ever-changing, these informal meeting-groups exist in every corner of the UK and can soon be tracked down. If you draw a blank in your area why not start one yourself? For those who regularly deal with clients on a personal consultation basis the question of insurance should also be considered, and some of the organisations listed here can advise on this, or may include such insurance cover in their membership fee.

Because the subject of astrology is such a wide umbrella—one might be a highly-paid media broadcaster or a book and calendar illustrator, or a healer or a phone-line consultant—or all of these (and more)—the rules and skills of your particular expertise may link in to other organisations that carry their own training and support programmes. However, the following addresses are specifically concerned with astrology in all its forms:

The Astrological Association,
Lee Valley Technopark,
Tottenham Hale,
London N17 9LN England
Tel: 0208 880 4848
Fax: 0208 880 4849
Email: astrological.association@zetnet.co.uk
Website: www.AstrologicalAssociation.com

The Astrological Lodge of London
50, Gloucester Place,
London
W1H 4EA
England
Website: www.astrolodge.co.uk

The Urania Trust
BCM Urania,
London
WC1N 3XX
England
Tel: 0171 700 0639
Email: urania@globalnet.co.uk
Website: www.uraniatrust.org

The Association of Professional Astrologers,
(The Secretary) Flat 12, Hermits Court,
Edinburgh
EH8 9RF
Scotland
Tel: 0800 0746113
Website: www.professionalastrologers.org

British Astrological and Psychic Society,
P.O.Box 363,
Rochester
ME1 3DJ
England
Tel: 0906 4700827
Fax: 01634 323006
Email: infi@baps.ws
Website: www.baps.ws

The Company of Astrologers,
P.O.Box 3001,
London
N1 1LY
England
Tel: 01227 362427
Email: admin@coa.org.uk
Website: www.hubcom.com/coa

British Association for Vedic Astrology,
1, Greenwood Close,
Romsey,
Hampshire
SO51 7QT
England
Tel: 01794 524178
Email: bava@btinternet.com
Website: www.bava.org

(Details of local groups and schools can be found at the Urania Trust website)

Astrology in Australia by Scott Whitters

One of the major issues for practising astrologers is having the profession identified and recognised as valid on a par with other professions, both within and from outside the industry. In a number of countries other than Australia, astrological bodies have formed which serve to promote and represent the practitioner who is making their living through astrology, whether this is through teaching, consulting, writing, researching or providing services to the astrological industry itself. At the time of publication, no such independent body representing the practising astrologer has been incorporated in Australia.

We are individually responsible for our own level of professionalism because the industry is self-regulating. However, the lack of professional representation and standing within the business community affects the psyche of the practicing astrological community as a whole. For an astrology practise to attain validation as a viable small business, the springboard is through adopting good business practices.

Michael E. Gerber (*The E-Myth Revisited*; 1995; Harper Business) has identified three hats that a small business operator must wear to fulfill the roles in a successful small business: the Technician, the Entrepreneur and the Manager. The Technician is the doer; in our sense the actual astrologer who sits down with a client, who leads the class in discussion or who writes the article for publication. The Entrepreneur sees opportunity around every corner, dreaming, driving, questing. The Manager, much maligned or ignored, is pragmatic, keeping records, implementing practices and procedures that keep order and manageability in the business. It is to the Manager that this chapter is primarily directed.

The first thing, from a business perspective, that an Australian astrologer needs to sort out is Taxation. From this, other important issues flow. In July 2000, the Australian Government implemented a major overhaul of the taxation system with the introduction of the Goods and Services Tax (GST). This has put added strain on small business due to the reporting requirements. A common complaint about the GST is that is forces small business holders to become tax collectors on behalf of the Government through the legal obligation of periodic reporting and payments. This, in a sense, does happen; however there has been a beneficial offshoot of this requirement - it has forced small business operators to keep their financial accounts up to date. Instead of reporting to the Taxation Office once a year, small business must now report at least five times a year; quarterly for GST purposes (through completion of a BAS or Business Activity Statement) and once for income tax purposes. It has served an additional purpose in identifying the backyard operator, running a purely cash in hand business to the detriment of those who set up in a proper manner.

The Taxation Office provides small businesses with a number of alternative approaches to Taxation compliance. For astrologers, the most fundamental is whether one classifies oneself as a professional or hobbyist. As a hobbyist, the astrologer practices without the intention of making a substantial profit or declaring a substantial profit. Because many payments can be cash payments, declaration of income may not always reflect the true cash flow situation. There is a major difference between tax minimalisation (which is legal) and tax avoidance (which is not).

There are several issues that make understating or not declaring one's income less attractive. Firstly, unless one can claim dependency on another person (which will also raise a series of personal issues), the Taxation Office will eventually demand to know where one's income is being generated. Similarly, when one comes to apply for various loans or lines of credit, the financial institution will require the previous three years business statements. If none of these show a return of substantial profit, then the institution will be less willing to part with their cash. The astrologer gets caught in a situation where opportunities for business and material growth and consolidation (just as important as spiritual, emotional and intellectual) are stunted.

The Taxation Office lists a number of factors that separate a business from a hobby. Some of these, in a sense, serve as business affirmations:

Does your activity have a significant commercial purpose or character?
Do you have a purpose of profit as well as a prospect of profit?
Is your activity planned, organised and carried on in a business-like manner?

If the astrologer should question any of these statements with regards to their business, then they would need to consider their intention to practise as a professional. Being a professional astrologer means to use astrology to earn a living and to charge a reasonable fee for services. As a professional it is insufficient to assume that the universe will provide. It won't. Success is most likely assured through effort and having a business structure set up and maintained. The Tax Office paradigms are a good basis for a business philosophy.

Embracing a business structure provides a trellis up which business can grow. It necessarily must have a Saturnian quality to it that doesn't have to equate to tedium. Saturn provides the matrix and thus, safety. Business structure does not ensure business longevity but it is pretty much impossible without it. It is the role of the Manager to operate within this framework. It is the role of the Entrepreneur to develop the business in such a way that the structure grows and develops along with it.

The three primary business structures adopted by astrologers are the Sole Trader, the Partnership and the Company.

The Sole Trader is the lone astrologer basing the business on individual control, management and remunerated effort. The Sole trader uses their individual Tax File Number when lodging an income tax return.

The Partnership is a recognised association of more than one person contributing time, effort and money to the business, assuming shared responsibilities and expecting profit. The Partnership lodges its income tax return under its own Tax File Number.

A Company is a legal entity, whether incorporated or not. It is expected to have its own Tax File Number and is regulated by the Australian Securities and Investments Commission (ASIC), to which it has a number of reporting requirements.

All businesses, regardless of their format, need to register for an Australian Business Number (ABN). The ABN is an identifying number that is used in all financial and commercial transactions with other businesses and in certain dealings with the Taxation Office and other government bodies. If you supply another business or individual with goods or services and do not quote your ABN, the other entity is obliged to withhold 48.5% of the invoiced total and forward this amount to the Taxation Office.

Although it is pretty much compulsory to apply for an ABN to run a business, it is not compulsory to register for GST unless one's annual turnover is $50,000 or more. However, even if it is anticipated that the annual turnover will be less than this, registering for GST is a sound business practice. Without registration, one cannot claim back from the Tax Office the amount of GST paid on goods and services for the business. By registering, the business becomes a part in the supply chain through which the GST is passed on to the final destination, the consumer. Without registering, the cost of the GST finally rests with the small business operator.

Irrespective of whether one is registered for GST, one is required by law to charge GST, on most goods and all services. There are quite severe penalties for not doing so, as there are for charging GST and not passing it on to the Tax office. At the time of publication, GST rate is a flat 10%. The GST charged and collected must be passed on to the Australian Taxation Office quarterly, with one's Business Activity Statement. This process, for astrologers, is fairly simple:

The amount of GST charged and collected is tallied.

The amount of GST paid is also tallied and subtracted from the GST charged.

If the GST charged is more than the GST paid, the remaining amount is forwarded to the Tax Office. This shows that a profit has been made for that quarter. If the amount collected is less than the amount paid, the small business operator can claim this difference back from the Tax Office. This shows that a loss was made for that quarter.

The Business Activity Statement comes as both a paper form and in electronic format. Initially, there were problems with the electronic format and mine never worked properly, so I have always completed the manual form. Irrespective of the reporting method, the calculations have to be performed manually. They are fairly straightforward. The form takes a few minutes to fill out and, because I am expecting to forward a cheque to the Taxation Office anyway, putting the form in the envelope with the cheque takes no extra effort.

As noted previously, this regular reporting requirement means that business accounts are not neglected for too long. It also means that one's accounting system needs to record three figures: the full amount charged or paid, the non-GST component and the component that represented the GST. Any accounting system, whether it is manual or electronic, needs to have the capability to record all three figures. All business invoices must also detail the GST component of any amount charged.

All of this information serves as a guide and should not replace advice received from the Australian Taxation Office or a Certified Practising Accountant. The Complete Tax Guide for Small Business is available free from the Australian Taxation Office, and is an excellent primary resource in familiarising oneself with the basic taxation obligations of small business. It also outlines how to apply for a business name and registration, an Australian Business Number and how to register for GST.

The Taxation Office operates two major internet sites:

www.ato.gov.au which is the main Taxation Office website detailing publications, tax rulings and other general information for small business; and

www.taxreform.ato.gov.au that deals specifically with the New Tax System introduced on 1 July 2000. It also contains TAXinteractive which is an online training facility introducing Taxation Office products for small business.

Another government resource is the Department of Employment, Workplace Relations and Small Business who co-ordinate the New Enterprise Incentive Scheme (NEIS) through which a person receives small business training and income support for the first 12 months of operation. Certain criteria apply. This option can be explored through www.dewrsb.gov.au

Generally, there are no licensing requirements in Australia for astrologers to practise. However, if one is proposing to establish an office, it is wise to check zoning regulations with the local council. This is merely a precaution.

The astrology industry is self-regulated without an effective, independent or representative regulating body. Due to this, there are no standards of practice. This has caused difficulty for astrologers in acquiring affordable Professional Indemnity Insurance. Because of the cost of the insurance, many astrologers are not covered. This applies also for more affordable insurance including Public Liability Insurance, Income Protection Insurance and, akin to this, Superannuation. Insurance and superannuation are easily forgotten and are usually one of the first things to be ignored when one is establishing a practice and cash flow is tight. These are all factors that should be addressed in a sound business plan.

Professional Indemnity Insurance has been a major issue of debate among practising astrologers and moves are afoot to organise an appropriate representative body to address this and other issues of concern to the practising astrologer. Currently, the organised astrological body within Australia is the Federation of Australian Astrologers (FAA). Branches are active in most States. However, whilst having some practising astrologers as its members, it is primarily comprised of hobbyists. Irrespective of this, the FAA serves as a good point of social contact to the astrological community. Contact details can be found under *Astrologers* in the Yellow Pages in each State. For the individual astrologer who is establishing a legal business, there are several identified and financially successful businesses operating in Australia, and in the main, the proprietors of these businesses are willing advisors.

Chapter Twelve

Epilogue

While writing this book, I have passed through many moods and memories. It has been very emotional for me to share, in such a personal and visceral way, all that I have gone through during this last Jupiter cycle as a self-employed astrologer. I wanted you, dear reader, *to feel what I lived,* rather than just reading my words. I have downloaded my hard drive and told you everything. Now I am free.

My intention for writing this book was to provide a practical blueprint of success for the astrology student just entering into a professional practice. Another goal of mine was to offer my colleagues a good read about the experience of being self-employed as an astrologer. I hope you had some good laughs, shed some tears, and found a comforting and validating parallel to your efforts through my story.

If astrologers start, build and grow practices, schools, mail-order businesses and publishing companies as a result of this book, then I will have done my job well. I hope to hear from any of you who take my business model and make it a success.

We are standing at the edge of history just now, as this planet of ours convulses in the dark days of the present Saturn-Pluto opposition. The role of the astrologer in modern times is growing, and will continue to do so, as people search for answers and perspective about the turbulent changes they are going through in response to global events of such magnitude. We have a sacred duty to comfort them.

I hope that the days of contention amongst astrologers will now cease. Shortly, our ruling planet of truth and awakening, Uranus, will ingress into Pisces. It will be an opportunity for astrologers everywhere to experience unity and solidarity. I ask you to climb on board this train, loving and respecting your colleagues.

The Joys & Rewards of Practicing & Teaching Astrology

I have worried over the tone of this book, not wanting to paint a portrait of self-employment as an astrologer that looks like a battlefield in a war zone. I also did not want to portray myself as an astrologer who was hardened by one too many heartaches. Truth is freedom, and I chose to be honest about my experiences.

There is a great joy for me in being an astrologer. This calling has been with me since I was 18 years old. I could not ever have known what it would take to get from there to here, but I would do it all over again tomorrow. When you hear your soul call to you, and you choose to listen and act on this inner voice, you become your authentic self. A deep peace emerges, and this peace guides you forward.

Despite all the challenges to building my business, and all of the stresses of financial uncertainty, this journey has made me a better human being, taught me much about life, and opened my heart.

The great reward for practicing and teaching astrology is the contribution that you make in the lives of others. With my eleventh house South Node, I came to this earth with a deep love of knowledge. My career as an astrologer has ushered me into my fifth house North Node, giving me a strong experience of love. When I use astrology to help someone in their life, I am helping them to regenerate through my love. When I teach someone the knowledge of astrology so as to enable them to help others, I am giving them an opportunity to share love. This is a good thing.

Our profession has been ridiculed, attacked, condemned and torched by those who are either ignorant, fearful, hypocritical or cruelly evil. Each time I represent astrology with dignity and professionalism to my clients and students, I stare down any derogators who would denounce us. My love for astrology is more powerful than the twisted hatred in their minds, and I will never fear them.

Solidarity: Why Self-Employed Astrologers Need One Another

When you are poor and broke, the whole world looks mean and ugly. In your mind you are just worrying about how you are going to cover your rent, buy groceries, and pay your bills. It is understandable, then, why self-employed astrologers have such scarcity fears, problems with self-esteem, and undervalue the worth of their services. I want to change that with my book. I visualize an institutional structure that supports the financial well-being and hard work of professional astrologers.

I realize that my experiences as a self-employed astrologer might have been harder than it will be for you. It is understandable that, with my second house Saturn, I may have had to struggle more than the average astrologer. Additionally, with my second house Neptune, it is quite clear to me that my financial boat may have a few more leaks in its hull than yours. I wish you prosperity, and I give you my prayers.

With all of the discussion today about ethics, education and certification, you certainly don't need any more from me. I would rather see pragmatic training for astrologers to build practices, attract clients, market their services, and become financially prosperous. I also want to see more emotional support and mutual understanding existing between astrologers.

How can this be done? In my mind, it will start with attitude and intention. As Uranus enters Pisces, we will have the opportunity to *think solidarity.* Sing a little song in your heart, *"We are one."* Turn off your computer, call a fellow astrologer in your hometown and ask how they are doing, if they are making enough money, and would it be OK to refer clients to them someday? Form a peer review group, share marketing ideas, and start a monthly salon where you speak in public.

A rising tide lifts all boats. The more you share with your fellow astrologers, the more your own practice and life will be blessed. Sound too idealistic? Just try it.

Remaining Loyal to Your Inner Light

Have you ever been asked, *"When are you going to get a real job?"* All astrologers will hear this at least once during their careers. Personally, I have a rock for a head, and I would rather die of poverty than go back to employment. To remain loyal to your inner light is a great accomplishment in life, and I admire you for your desire and aspiration to practice astrology. You have my respect.

Your truth will set you free. If it is your truth to be an astrologer, *do it.* The money will come, the bills will get paid, the love and support will be there, and your own heart will grow strong and endure all tests and obstacles. I truly hope that this book will encourage you to go for it, and help you in a practical way to get organized and write a business plan that will make you a living as an astrologer.

Your inner light is your power and strength. It comes straight from your heart. No person can take this away from you. If you step into this light, it will protect you, provide for you, and guide you forward as an astrologer. Believe in this Light.

Appendix I

Contact Information for Local Astrology Groups
[please e-mail the publisher at ewastro@earthlink.net with any revisions, additions or deletions]

USA

Cape Ann School of Astrology • PO Box 7092 • Gloucester MA 01930

Mandalay West Astrology Center • 32 Benton Ave. • Barrington MA 02134

NCGR Boston Chapter • 209 Common St. • Belmont MA 02478

NCGR Cape Cod Chapter • PO Box 613 • Harwich Port MA 02636

New Hampshire Astrological Association • PO Box 3088 • Manchester NH 03105

Seacoast Astrological Association • PO Box 4683 • Portsmouth NH 03802

Astrology Association of Connecticut • 290 Nevers Rd. • South Windsor CT 06079

Astrological Society of Connecticut • PO Box 290346 • Wethersfield CT 06129

NCGR Berkshire-Fairfield Chapter • 297 Nod Hill Rd. • Wilton CT 06897

NCGR Northern New Jersey Chapter • 10 Sutherland Rd. • Montclair NJ 07042

Delaware Valley Astrological Society • 321 Cedar Lane • Racocas Woods NJ 08073

Cosmic Circle Astrological Association • 1160 Hurffville Rd • Deptford NJ 08096

Astrological Society of Princeton • 173/175 Harrison St. • Princeton NJ 08540

Church of Light Brotherhood • 1565 Alamitos Dr. • Lakewood NJ 08701

NCGR New York City Chapter • 319 W. 19th St. • New York NY 10011

Wise Kings Astrological Association • PO Box 348 • Brooklyn NY • 11239

NCGR Long Island Chapter • 8 Eustace Dr. • Commack NY 11725

NCGR Mid Hudson Chapter • 3140 Rt. 209 #6H • Kingston NY 12401

NCGR Upstate New York Chapter • 272 Hickory Hill Rd. • Fort Plain NY 13339

Astral Club of Western New York • PO Box 1210 • Buffalo NY 14213

Astrosophia • 6210 Sellers St. • Pittsburgh PA 15206

Pittsburgh Astrology Association • 815 Copeland St. • Pittsburgh PA 15232

Harrisburg Astrological Society • 3812 Hearthstone Rd. • Camp Hill PA 17011

Lehigh Valley Astrological Society • PO Box 453 • Coopersburg PA • 18036

Osaka University of Astrological Sciences • PO Box 768 • Canadensis PA 18325

NCGR Greater Delaware Valley Chapter • PO Box 842 • West Chester PA 19381

Philadelphia Astrological Society • PO Box 502 • Lansdowne PA 19050

NCGR Metro Washington Chapter • PO Box 42691 • Washington DC 20015

Washington Astrology Forum • 737 Easley St. • Silver Spring MD 20910

NCGR Baltimore Chapter • 116 Nunnery Lane #D • Catonsville MD 21228

NCGR Annapolis Chapter • 7934 Roxbury Drive • Glen Burnie MD 21061

Astrological Association of Northern Virginia • PO Box 1521 • Vienna VA 22183

NCGR Richmond Chapter • PO Box 8412 • Richmond VA 23226

Virginia Astrological Association • 3403 Horse Way • Virginia Beach VA 23452

Astrology-Graphology Study Group • PO Box 2964 • Virginia Beach VA 23454

NCGR Raleigh-Durham Chapter • 211 Montibello Dr. • Cary NC 27513

NCGR Queen Charlotte Chapter • 2625 Bucknell Ave. • Charlotte NC 28207

NCGR Carolina's Chapter • PO Box 9211 • Greenville SC 29604

NCGR Atlanta Chapter • 490 Broadland Rd. NW • Atlanta GA 30342

Metro Atlanta Astrological Society • PO Box 451123 • Atlanta GA 30345

North Florida Astrological Association • PO Box 1741 • Jacksonville FL 32201

Astrological Research Guild, Inc. • PO Box 52 • Goldenrod FL 32733

Florida Astrological Association • 1712 Lake Downey Dr. • Union Park FL 32807

NCGR Central Florida Chapter • 1070 Leeway Ct. • Orlando FL 32810

South Florida Astrological Association • 10240 Dolphin Rd. • Miami FL 33157

NCGR Florida Atlantic Chapter • PO Box 4991 • Deerfield Beach FL 33442

Suncoast Astrological Group • 6822 22nd Ave. N. #110 • St. Petersburg FL 33710

Astrological Association of St. Petersburg • 11325 88th Ave. N. • Seminole FL 33772

NCGR Paradise Found Chapter • 5000 Burnt Store Rd. • Punta Gorda FL 33955

NCGR Nashville Chapter • 3918 Dorcas Drive • Nashville TN 37215

Riverside Astrologers • 5548 Lyford St. • Memphis TN 38117

Astrological Society of Kentucky • 3317 Goldsmith Lane • Louisville KY 40220

Ohio Valley Society of Astrologers • 825 Leiber St. • Henderson KY 42420

Toledo Area Astrological Society • 3232 River Rd. • Toledo OH 43614

Lake County Astrological Association • 8715 Mentor Ave. • Mentor OH 44060

Cuyahoga Astrological Research Association • PO Box 553 • Lakewood OH 44107

Quest Astrological Research • 753 Brayton Ave. • Cleveland OH 44113

Ohio Astrological Association • 14755 Drexmore Rd • Shaker Heights OH 44120

WRAC • 9670 Pleasant Lakes #Y-40 • Parma OH 44130

Akron Astrological Society • PO Box 5723 • Akron OH 44327

Mahoning Valley Astrological Association • PO Box 118 • Mineral Ridge OH 44440

Astrological Forum of Dayton • 4309 Natchez Ave. • Dayton OH 45416

Indiana Federation of Astrologers • 2341 Barnor Dr. • Indianapolis IN 46219

Ohio Valley Astrological Society • 856 So. Kentucky Ave. • Newburgh IN 47630

PAR • 48660 Callens • New Baltimore MI 48047

Michigan Federation of Astrologers • 4907 Eastlawn Dr. • Lansing MI 48910

Western Michigan Cosmic Astrologers • PO Box 88323 • Kenwood MI 49518

Astrology Club of Cedar Rapids • 1253 Hazel Dr. NE • Cedar Rapids IA 52402

Milwaukee Astrology Center • 4556 No. 704th St. • Milwaukee WI 53218

NCGR Milwaukee Chapter • 265 No. 110th St. • Milwaukee WI 53226

NCGR STARS Chapter • 1359 Sargent Ave. • St. Paul MN 55128

NCGR Northern Illinois Chapter • 29W100 Butterfield Rd. #103 • Warrenville IL 60009

NCGR SW Suburban Chapter • 12604 Kinvarra Dr. • Palos Park IL 60464

Friends of Astrology • 535 Woodside Ave. • Hinsdale IL 60521

NCGR Chicago Chapter • 912 Woolf Ct. • Rochelle IL 61068

The Aquarian Society • 303 East Wilson Ave. • Machesney IL 61115

Astrological Association of St. Louis • PO Box 16282 • Clayton MO 63105

NCGR St. Louis Chapter • 612 Cleveland Ave. • Kirkwood MO 63122

Aquarian Organization of Astrologers • PO Box 36493 • Kansas City MO 64111

Unisight Foundation • PO Box 2 • Lansing KS 66043

NCGR Oklahoma City Chapter • PO Box 12085 • Oklahoma City OK 73157

Tulsa Astrological Society • PO Box 54515 • Tulsa OK 74155

East Texas Astrological Association • Route 2, Box 25-A • Grapeland TX 75844

Astrological Society of Fort Worth • PO Box 126062 • Benbrook TX 76126

NCGR Gulf Coast Chapter • 1100 Augusta #63 • Houston TX 77057

North Houston Astrological Association • PO Box 90036 • Houston TX 77090

STARS • PO Box 200496 • San Antonio TX 78220

El Paso Astrology Association • 1508 Oakdale • El Paso TX 79927

NCGR Rocky Mountain Chapter • PO Box 328 • Rollinsville CO 80474

Friends of Metaphysics • 10623 Van Gordon Way • Broomfield CO 80020

Colorado Federation of Astrologers • 999 So. Clermont • Denver CO 80202

Colorado Fellowship of Astrologers • 700 Washington St. #402 • Denver CO 80203

Astrology Association of Colorado Sgs • 2209 W Colorado Ave. • Colorado Springs CO 80902

Astrological Society of Utah • 1085 N. Garnette Circle • Salt Lake City UT 84116

Arizona Society of Astrologers • PO Box 9340 • Scottsdale AZ 85252

Tucson Astrologers Guild • 3311 S. Whistler Dr. • Tucson AZ 85730

NCGR Red Rock Chapter • 125 Rainbow Rock Rd. • Sedona AZ 86351

NCGR Enchantment Chapter • 721 Jefferson NE • Albuquerque NM 87110

Astrology Forum • PO Box 22607 • Santa Fe NM 87502

NCGR Stargazers Chapter • 6233 Bellota #D • Las Vegas NV 89108

Las Vegas Astrologer's Roundtable • 5029 Celebrity Circle • Las Vegas NV 89119

ISAR Southern Nevada Chapter • 3430 E. Flamingo Rd. #250 • Las Vegas NV 89121

NCGR Los Angeles County Chapter • 6333 Canoga Ave. #391 • Woodland Hills CA 91367

California Astrology Association • PO Box 810 • North Hollywood CA 91603

Astrology Society of Southern California • PO Box 642 • Glendora CA 91740

NCGR San Diego Chapter • 1426 Coronado Ave. • Spring Valley CA 91977

Unisight • PO Box 903 • La Jolla CA 92038

San Diego Astrological Society • PO Box 16430 • San Diego CA 92116

Western States Astrological Research • PO Box 1083 • Newport Beach CA 92663

Southern California Astrological Network • 11 Gema • San Clemente CA 92672

Phoenix Society of the Pacific • 590 Wadsworth Ave. • Pismo Beach CA 93449

Antelope Valley Astrology Club • 2553 East Palmdale Blvd. #L • Palmdale CA 93550

NCGR Bay Area Chapter • PO Box 4834 • Mountain View CA 94040

Institute for Stellar Influence Studies • 4482-B Appian Way • El Sobrante CA 94803

South Bay Astrological Society • 43 Montgomery St. • Los Gatos CA 95030

NCGR Sacramento Chapter • 10227 Fair Oaks Blvd. • Sacramento CA 95628

NCGR Hawaii Chapter • 98-850B Iho Place • Aiea HI 96701

Oregon Astrological Association • PO Box 6771 • Portland OR 97228

Eugene Astrology Salon • 718 E. 21st Ave. • Eugene OR 97405

NCGR Southern Oregon Chapter • PO Box 1049 • Ashland OR 97520

Astrology-Get-Together • 915 East Pine St. #401 • Seattle WA 98122

Washington State Astrological Association • PO Box 45386 • Seattle WA 98145

Astrologers of the North • 621 King Arthur Circle • Anchorage AK 99518

CANADA

Ottawa Astrological Society • 1002-31 McEwen Ave. • Ottawa Ontario K2B 5K6

Astrology Toronto, Inc. • http://www.astrology-toronto-inc.com/

Niagara Frat. of Astrologers • 6292 Brookfield Ave. • Niagara Falls Ontario L2G 5R8

Manitoba Assoc. of Astrologers • #201-237 Wellington Cr. • Winnipeg Manitoba R3M 0A1

Calgary Astrological Association • Box 30431 • Calgary Alberta T2H 2W1

The Fraser Valley Astrological Guild • Box 833 • Fort Langley BC V1M 2S2

Vancouver Society of Astrologers • #8-1786 Esquimalt Ave • West Vancouver BC V7V 1R8

Appendix II

Lecture, Class & Workshop Tapes by the Author

Vision '94 Conference San Diego • **"Solar System Model of Planetary Consciousness"** • Lecture $8.95

Vision '94 Conference San Diego • **"Partners Who Activate Our Shadow"** • Lecture $8.95

UAC'95 Conference Monterey • **"Multiple Levels of the Outer Planets"** • Lecture $8.95

Astrological Conference of Western Canada 1996 • **"Secondary Progressions"** • Lecture $8.95

Astrological Conference of Western Canada 1997 • **"The Ascendant"** • Lecture $8.95

Vancouver Society of Astrologers 1999 • **"Foundations of Progression Theory"** • Lecture $10.95

ISAR 2000 • **"Progression Theory & Transit Triggers"** • Lecture $8.95

ISAR 2000 • **"Secondary, Tertiary & Minor Progressed Client Counseling"** • Lecture $8.95

Astrological Conference of Western Canada 1997 • **"Astrology & Anger"** • Workshop (2 tapes) $14.95
Examines the four patterns of anger as defined by the stressful aspects to Mars, Saturn, Uranus & Pluto

Earthwalk Astrology 1998 • **"Neptune in Aquarius (1998-2012)"** • Workshop (2 tapes) $14.95
Previous Neptune in Aquarius periods (1506-1520, 1670-1684, 1834-1848); plus generational effect

Earthwalk Astrology 1998 • **"The Ascendant"** • Workshop (2 tapes) $14.95
12 versions of each rising sign; chart ruler; prog. ascendant; transits to the ascendant; Sabian symbols

Earthwalk Astrology 1998 • **"Karmic Astrology"** • Workshop (2 tapes) $14.95
Nodes; retrograde planets; twelfth house; interceptions; eclipses; ascendant; the Moon; Saturn; Pluto

Earthwalk Astrology 1998 • **"Jupiter & Saturn"** • Workshop (2 tapes) $14.95
Realms of social and spiritual involvement; by sign, house, aspect, house rulership, transit and prog.

Earthwalk Astrology 1998 • **"Transforming Loss to Gain"** • Workshop (2 tapes) $14.95
Pluto; Scorpio; 8th house; loss, death and renewal in life; emotionally ravaged soul coming back to life

Earthwalk Astrology 1998 • **"The Lunar Nodes"** • Workshop (2 Tapes) $14.95
Patterns from past lives; soul purpose; transiting nodes; nodes in synastry and composite charts

Earthwalk Astrology 1998 • **"Electional Astrology"** • Workshop (2 Tapes) $14.95
Techniques for picking a wedding date; scheduling medical surgery; starting a business & more

Earthwalk Astrology 1999 • **"Esoteric Astrology"** • Workshop (2 Tapes) $14.95
Spiritual meanings of the different levels of planetary intelligence revealed to us through their glyphs

Earthwalk Astrology 1999 • **"Sabian Aspect Orbs"** • Workshop (2 Tapes) $14.95
Sabian Symbols define angular separation between planets; waxing, waning, applying and separating

Earthwalk Astrology 1999 • **"Sabian Symbols"** • Workshop (2 Tapes) $14.95
Origin and history; significant natal degrees; meaningful current progressed degrees

Earthwalk Astrology 1999 • **"Medical Astrology"** • Workshop (2 Tapes) $14.95
Constitutional analysis; body-mind connection; planetary weakness; Yods; hard natal aspects

San Diego Astrological Society 2001 • **"Progressions Workshop"** • Workshop (3 tapes) $14.95
Secondary, Tertiary & Minor inter-relationship with natal & transits; lunations; retrogradation; stations

ARG of Orlando 2001 • **"Partners Who Activate Our Shadow"** • Workshop (3 tapes) $14.95
Karmic relationship theory; relationship as transformation; Chiron and healing dimensions of love

Astrology: A Language of Life • **Complete Set of Seven Two-Hour Beginning Class Tapes $69.95**
Week 1: Elements, Modes & Zodiac Signs • Week 2: Planets • Week 3: Houses • Week 4: Aspects I
Week 5: Aspects II • Week 6: Planetary Patterns & Aspect Configurations • Week 7: Chart Synthesis

Chart Interpretation Handbook by Stephen Arroyo • **Beginning Class Textbook $10.95**

Intermediate Astrology Class • **Complete Set of Eight Two-Hour Class Tapes $89.95**
Week 1: Retrogrades • Week 2: Transits • Week 3: Progressions • Week 4: Lunar Nodes & Life Purpose
Week 5: Relationship Analysis Techniques • Week 6: Aspects & 360° Cycle Analysis
Week 7: Solar Returns • Week 8: House Rulerships & Dispositors

Class Tapes Include Handouts, Reading Assignments, Written Essays & Recommended Book List

To Order by Mail or Phone:

Add $1 postage per lecture; $2.00 per workshop; or $5.20 per class up to maximum $8 postage

Earthwalk School of Astrology PO Box 832 Ashland OR 97520 USA 1.800.778.8490
ewastro@earthlink.net • MasterCard/VISA accepted • e-mail for a postage quotation abroad

Appendix III
Astrology Software Programs

For Windows

Solar Fire 5: The Complete Professional Calculation Program   call for current price
[includes *ACS PC Atlas:* American & International]
Solar Maps: Relocation Interpretations; Eclipse Paths   call for current price
JigSaw 2: Rectification; Research; Family Patterns   call for current price

For Macintosh

Io Edition: The Complete Professional Calculation Program   call for current price
Star*Sprite: Time Machine; Research; Event Searching; Color Charts   call for current price
Io Detective: Search Chart Files For Like Criteria (signs, houses, aspects)   call for current price
Io Atlas: American & International Atlas For Macintosh   call for current price
Io Series Interpreters: Io Horoscope (natal); Io Forecast (transits);
Io Relationship (synastry & composite)   call for current price
Specially Priced Packages: Multiple Programs @ Substantial Savings   call for current price

To Order Programs or Request Catalogues

call or write

Earthwalk School of Astrology
PO Box 832
Ashland OR 97520 USA
1.800.778.8490
ewastro@earthlink.net

MasterCard/VISA accepted

Appendix IV
Computer Chart Services

Natal Chart + Data Page

Yearly Progressed Hit List

Monthly Transit Search (Sun thru Mars)

90° or 360° Midpoint Sort

Natal/Transit Bi-Wheel

Lunar Return (Standard or Precessed)

Synastry Table (Interchart Aspects)

Composite Chart

Yearly Transit Search (Mars thru Pluto)

Progressed Chart

6-Month Graphic Ephemeris

Natal/Progressed/Transit Tri-Wheel

Solar Return (Standard or Precessed)

End of Life Chart

Time-Space Relationship Chart

Lifetime Secondary Lunations

1 or 2 charts ordered - $5.00 ea. • 3 or more charts ordered - $4.00 ea. + $1.00 postage/order

Lifetime Tertiary Lunations   Lifetime Minor Lunations

$10.00 ea. + $1.00 postage

Complete Natal Chart Sabian Aspect Orb Summary

includes every angular separation between all planets along with corresponding Sabian Symbols

call for price

Specify Options

House Division System: Placidus   Koch   Equal   Porphyry   Campanus   Natural

Planets/Chiron/Asteroids: Planets Only   Planets & Chiron   Planets, Asteroids & Chiron

Aspect Lines: Ptolemaic Only (Conjunction, Sextile, Square, Trine, Opposition)

Add Quincunxes; Add Semi-Squares; Add Sesquiquadrates; No Aspect Lines (Hub Chart)

Chartwheel Style: American (houses equally sized)   European (houses shown in actual size)

Lunar Nodes: True Node   Mean Node

Other Options: Add Part of Fortune   Add Node Aspects   Add ASC & MC Aspects

To Order Charts

call or write

Earthwalk School of Astrology
PO Box 832
Ashland OR 97520 USA
1.800.778.8490
ewastro@earthlink.net

MasterCard/VISA accepted

Appendix V
Contacting The Author

To Write The Author

Correspondence may be sent to:

Earthwalk School of Astrology
PO Box 832
Ashland OR 97520 USA
ewastro@earthlink.net

Author Availability For Lectures/Workshops

Mr. Blaschke is available to lecture and teach workshops
on many astrological techniques and topics.

To request lecture/workshop synopses for your local astrological association,
conference faculty or symposium, please write the publisher.

Author Availability For Telephone Consultation

Mr. Blaschke is available for personal consultation over the telephone. One-hour
phone consultation appointments can be scheduled through the publisher.
Call 1.800.778.8490 for appointment scheduling.

Bibliography

Astrology, Psychology & The Four Elements • Stephen Arroyo • CRCS • 1975

Astrology, Karma & Transformation • Stephen Arroyo • CRCS • 1978

Relationships & Life Cycles • Stephen Arroyo • CRCS • 1979

Chart Interpretation Handbook • Stephen Arroyo • CRCS • 1989

The Rulership Book • Rex E. Bills • Macoy Publishing • 1971

Astrology: A Language of Life; Volume I - Progressions
Robert P. Blaschke • Earthwalk School of Astrology • 1998

Astrology: A Language of Life; Volume II - Sabian Aspect Orbs
Robert P. Blaschke • Earthwalk School of Astrology • 2000

The Principles of Astrology • Charles E.O. Carter • Theosophical Publishing House • 1925

The Zodiac and the Soul • Charles E.O. Carter • Theosophical Publishing House • 1928

The Astrological Aspects • Charles E.O. Carter • Theosophical Publishing House • 1930

The Degrees of the Zodiac Symbolised • Charubel [John Thomas] • L.N. Fowler & Co. • 1898

Encyclopedia Of Astrology • Nicholas deVore • Philosophical Library • 1957

Skymates • Jodie & Steven Forrest • Seven Paws Press • 2002

Pluto: The Evolutionary Journey of the Soul • Jeff Green • Llewellyn • 1985

The Outer Planets & Their Cycles • Liz Greene • CRCS • 1983

Planets In Composite • Robert Hand • Whitford Press • 1975

Planets In Transit • Robert Hand • Whitford Press • 1976

Secondary Progressions • Nancy Hastings • Samuel Weiser • 1984

The Sabian Symbols in Astrology • Marc Edmund Jones • Aurora Press • 1993

The Progressed Horoscope • Alan Leo • Astrologer's Library • 1906

Esoteric Astrology • Alan Leo • L.N. Fowler & Co. Ltd. • 1967

Mars: the War Lord • Alan Leo • Samuel Weiser • 1970

Jupiter: the Preserver • Alan Leo • Samuel Weiser • 1970

Saturn: the Reaper • Alan Leo • Samuel Weiser • 1970

The Astrology of Self-Discovery • Tracy Marks • CRCS • 1985

The Art Of Chart Interpretation • Tracy Marks • CRCS • 1986

The Astrologer's Astronomical Handbook • Jeff Mayo • L.N. Fowler & Co. Ltd. • 1965

The Solar Return Book of Prediction • Raymond A. Merriman • Seek-It Publishing • 1977

Astrology, The Divine Science • Marcia Moore & Mark Douglas • Arcane • 1971

Planets In Houses • Robert Pelletier • Whitford Press • 1978

Modern Transits • Lois M. Rodden • AFA • 1978

An Astrological Mandala: The Cycle of Transformations and Its 360 Symbolic Phases
Dane Rudhyar • Random House • 1973

Cycles of Becoming • Alexander Ruperti • CRCS • 1978

Karmic Astrology, Volume I: The Moon's Nodes and Reincarnation
Martin Schulman • Samuel Weiser • 1975

Karmic Astrology, Volume II: Retrogrades & Reincarnation
Martin Schulman • Samuel Weiser • 1977

Karmic Relationships • Martin Schulman • Samuel Weiser • 1984

Dynamics Of Aspect Analysis • Bil Tierney • CRCS • 1983